I HAVE
—*The*—
POWER

I HAVE *The* POWER

Unlocking Your Potential to Change the World

NKANDU BELTZ

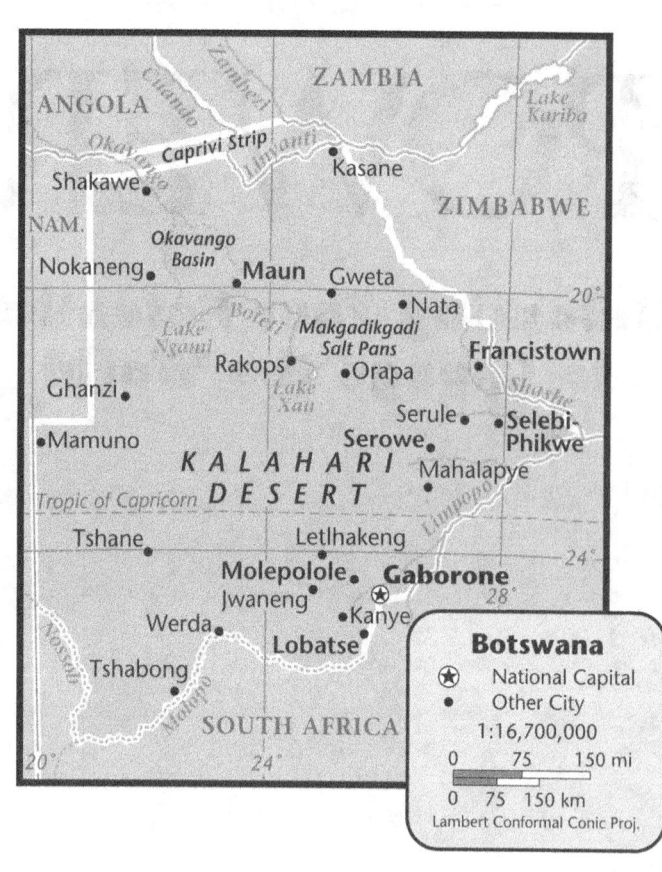

Words of Acknowledgment for Nkandu

> "As a member of the UNAAWA Executive team in 2011-12, Nkandu Beltz was a caring, committed advocate for young people and the disadvantaged, from both a local and global perspective. Based in Kununurra, she provided us with a distinctive perspective about issues and was passionate about human rights and making a practical difference. Nkandu's enthusiasm and ability to connect and communicate with people make her an influential agent for change."
>
> *Carolyne Gatward,*
>
> President, United Nations Association Australia
> (WA Division) Inc.

I Have the Power

> ❝ Nkandu Beltz is an inspiring young woman who very effectively advocated on behalf of the young people of Kununurra when she was living there, providing this Department and the Minister for Youth at the time with valuable insights into the local scene. She provided the impetus for local initiatives involving the youth of the area and brought about new levels of collaboration between the agencies involved. We greatly appreciated her commitment, wisdom and local netwosrking skills, which gave us access to someone fully involved in one of our most remote communities.
>
> *Stuart Reid,*
>
> Former Director Policy and Planning: Children, Youth and Families. Department of Communities, WA

> ❝ "Dear Nkandu,
>
> If I would use a word to describe today, I would describe it as "Empowering". Thank you for such a wonderful day and the amazing work you do. I felt at home today and I was glad. Your talk also affirmed my passions and my goals and displayed the incredible and outstanding person you are. So once again, I say "THANK YOU!' It was such an honour and privilege to meet you today.
>
> Regards,"
>
> *Whitney Ombega*

Words of Acknowledgment for Nkandu

> *Hey Nkandu,*
>
> *This is an essay I wrote for English class. It's about a show we watched called Brat camp. If you don't know what it is, it's about troubled and misbehaved teenagers who need help. Besides the point when I finished writing this essay I thought well I've had this for 24 hours and it's finished. I worked for a good 12 hours in the 24 hours I've had it and its only 849 words, that's a big effort for me, but then I realized I don't think I would have been able to finish it so quickly without the thought of your determination to have things completed on time. Nkandu, even though I may not see you for a little while, your values will stick with me throughout life and I thank you for that."*
>
> Tayla Jade, 16

I Have the Power

I Have The Power: Unlocking Your Potential to Change the World © Nkandu Beltz 2016.

www.ihavethepowerbook.com

www.nkandubeltz.com.au

The moral rights of Nkandu Beltz to be identified as the author of this work have been asserted in accordance with the Copyright Act 1968.

First published in Australia in 2014.

Second Edition 2016.

ISBN 978-0-9924977-3-6

Any opinions expressed in this work are exclusively those of the author.

All rights reserved. No part of this publication may be reproduced or transmitted by any means, electronic, photocopying or otherwise, without prior written permission of the author.

Disclaimer

All the information, techniques, skills and concepts contained within this publication are of the nature of general comment only, and are not in any way recommended as individual advice. The intent is to offer a variety of information to provide a wider range of choices now and in the future, recognising that we all have widely diverse circumstances and viewpoints. Should any reader choose to make use of the information herein, this is their decision, and the author and publisher/s do not assume any responsibilities whatsoever under any conditions or circumstances. The author does not take responsibility for the business, financial, personal or other success, results or fulfilment upon the readers' decision to use this information. It is recommended that the readers obtain their own independent advice.

Dedicated to YOU, to the
ones who have struggled
in their lives and to those
who wake up every morning
fighting to make this world a
better place.

Here's to the triumphs in life!

Rotary and the Change it Makes

Rotary began by one man who was lonely and wanted to meet and join a group of friends . Ever since that day Rotary has been changing lives locally, nationally and internationally. We have a saying in Rotary, that there are no strangers in Rotary , only friends that you have not met yet. What a wonderful way to impact the world – through greater diversity, greater knowledge , greater friendships and a greater understanding of humanity.

Rotary identified that greater world peace would be achieved by greater understanding. It soon developed peace scholarships around the world for post graduate study. Rotary clubs have been able to identify young students around the world as part of this program and provided financial support through our charity, The Rotary Foundation. Peace scholars have then gone on to work on peace initiatives throughout the world , in particular in areas of major conflict.

Youth Exchange is a program made available to students fifteen to eighteen years of age around the world , to enable them to experience short or long term exchange in a foreign country. This promotes international understanding of cultural and language diversity by allowing students to live as part of a family overseas – often taking them outside their comfort zone – and by challenging them to grow and mature as young adults. All students taking part of the program experience a life changing event – and many develop a taste for international travel and a future where they can give back to the communities that supported them on this journey.

Rotary also influences students in the 12 to 15 year age group by a program called Interact. This teaches them the value of community programs , volunteering and leadership skills – all fabulous life skills to make them be better prepared for adult life. Specific youth leadership programs are also run by Rotary Districts and provide week long camps (

I Have the Power

RYPEN – Rotary Youth Program of Enrichment) to young students from 15 to 18 years of age and concentrates on teamwork and developing team dynamics. RYLA – (Rotary Youth Leadership Awards) is designed for 18 to 30 year old adults to further develop their leadership qualities. Many companies send staff to such programs because they have identified the quality of speakers and mentors within the program. They have also seen the growth of individuals after completing these programs. Many participants of RYLA have gone on to be leaders of future programs – further embracing and developing their leadership qualities by providing support and engagement to the next generation of recipients.

Rotary itself is changing to be more flexible to the next generation of Rotarians. This means greater flexibility of club meeting times and identifying community service and social activities as meaningful ways of contributing to club participation. The ideal of Service Above Self is still the core value of Rotary around the world – with more focus on engagement of activities rather than simply on attendance.

For Rotary to continue to be relevant it must continue to adapt to a changing world. Rotary has been serving humanity and changing the world and lives since 1911 – and with support of the next generations it shall continue to do so .

Stephen Lamont

D9780

Contents

Foreword		1
Introduction		3
Chapter 1:	Born to be a Change-maker	7
Chapter 2:	A Country Childhood	19
Chapter 3:	From a Land of Kings and Queens	31
Chapter 4:	Drastic Confrontations	43
Chapter 5:	Becoming a Peer Educator	53
Chapter 6:	Moving Down Under	65
Chapter 7:	Honouring My Calling	83
Chapter 8:	Becoming an Official Young Social Pioneer	91
Chapter 9:	A Helicopter View	99
Chapter 10:	Dreams Continue to Come True	111
Chapter 11:	You are Perfect with Your Imperfections	119
Chapter 12:	Emotional Intelligence	131
Chapter 13:	Looking After Yourself Looks After the World	139
Chapter 14:	My Other Sources of Inspiration	145
Chapter 15:	STEMSEL	151
Chapter 16:	(Shikoba) I Exist For You	161
Chapter 17:	Nkandu's Cultural Night	173
Acknowledgments		187
About The Author		189

Foreword

As I read ***I Have the Power*** I was filled with a sense of awe: not only for the remarkable individual that is Nkandu Beltz, but for the strength and resilience of her family, her community and the vast and timeless continent in which she was born, Africa.

Nkandu often speaks of the African philosophy of Ubuntu. Archbishop Emeritus Desmond Tutu has said, "Ubuntu is very difficult to render into a Western language… It is to say 'My humanity is caught up, is inextricably bound up, in what is yours'".

This idea that we are inextricably entwined in each other's fate; that we are not, in fact, isolated, atomized individuals but part of a much larger collective is a powerful ideal which has resonance far beyond its African roots. You cannot read this book without an overwhelming experience of our common humanity. Our interconnectedness. Our Ubuntu.

Nkandu's journey as a child and young person in Africa, a young adult in the Netherlands and regional Australia could have been a story of a clash of cultures, values and beliefs. Instead, this exceptional story is of the struggle and power of 'becoming'. Of the journey to discovering oneself. The result is a young woman with the most extraordinary sense of self, grace and generosity.

Of course for many people that would be enough. For Nkandu, this is the foundation upon which her passion to empower others has been built. She has spent her life advocating for justice, contributing to building community and ensuring no one is left behind.

I Have the Power

Nkandu is part of a new generation of young, educated, global citizens who see and experience the world in its entirety. These young Changemakers believe we can all be, and do, better in the world. I have the immense privilege of backing their courage, imagination and will and witnessing their leadership and impact in my work with the Foundation for Young Australians.

As Archbishop Tutu goes on to say, "A person with Ubuntu is open and available to others, affirming of others, does not feel threatened that others are able and good, for he or she has a proper self-assurance that comes from knowing that he or she belongs in a greater whole and is diminished when others are humiliated or diminished, when others are tortured or oppressed."

Nkandu has shown us the way. She encourages young people to travel their own path, to find their purpose and meaning and to contribute. She inspires us all to own and share our stories, follow our passions and be the change we wish to see in the world.

Jan Owen AM

Chief Executive Officer

Foundation for Young Australians

Introduction

> *"Never underestimate what an individual with a powerful thought can do."*
>
> **Nkandu Beltz**

Have you ever woken up one day and thought to yourself that you wanted to change something? Well, I feel like that most of the time! The power of one is the most powerful concept I know. You have the ability to influence people and start a movement, which will benefit so many people right now, and perhaps generations to come later on. What is your definite purpose in life? Mine is to inspire people and bring out the best in everyone that I meet. I'm easy going and relaxed. I like to think that I have very good communication skills. I can talk with anyone. Leave me in the middle of Timbuktu and I'll make friends in two minutes, eating what the locals eat, and joining in their way of life.

I've been told that happiness is a choice. Stop waiting for problems to disappear in order for you to appreciate what you have in your life. You should never be terrified of making mistakes; that won't get you anywhere in life. One of the best things I like to do is write down what has happened in my day. This way, I look at the failures

I Have the Power

and triumphs. Then I treat these two the same; I take it as a lesson and I did what was best at that time.

When I was working for the Ngami Times, I went to report on the Airborne exercise that was held in Tsau, near Maun in Botswana. This was hard-core military training and I was in gear, wearing my jeans and combat shirt and carrying my media equipment. I was the only girl at the training ground, but I still felt powerful and strong! I was 18 years old. My role was to report on what was happening, even though I had male journalists intimidating me and pushing me to fly back home, as it was not safe. I was very adamant about staying to finish my task.

After four days, we went back to Maun and had a party at the Sedie Riverside Hotel. I had met Kevin Czarkowski, an American soldier. He was a very good sounding board and said some things to me I'll never forget. As we talked about life, love and work, he said to me, "Nkandu, 10% of life includes the physics of life. The other 90% is how you react to the situations around you." This is very true. We choose how to respond to events in our life. Sometimes, we think we can't help it and it's just easier to sit in our corner of the room and blame the world and complain how unfair this world is. The truth is, you can look at your mistakes, say, "Oh well, that was a stupid thing to do, but now I know better and will move on to the next thing." It's all about attitude. Your attitude determines your character as well as your success in life.

During my journey as a young social change-maker, I have come across many "self-help" books. This book is not one of them. This book is just a reminder that you are truly amazing and to encourage you to just believe in yourself. I have done a lot of work with young people, starting from my birth country, Zambia, in Botswana and a significant amount of my life in Australia.

Introduction

Africa was my stepping-stone, but the challenges that young people all over the world face are the same. It's the battle between who we are and who we want to be. Of course we do have other challenges in Africa, like the massive amount of unemployment and the PHDs (Poverty, Hunger and Disease) in some African countries. This book is a reminder that you are important and as an important member of this community your skills, knowledge and contribution is critical for the development of your country. You have a tremendous amount of skills and talents to share with the rest of the world. This requires having an open mind and an open heart, and then tapping into your inner being and unleashing your brilliance. Change has to start with you. Like Ghandi said, "Be the change you want to see in the world."

This book comes from my core being. Even now as I'm writing this, tears are trickling down my cheeks. It's such a privilege to share my journey and the lessons learned with you. These are lessons on the love of humanity, compassion, making change in my community, how other people live in other countries, and the celebration of cultural diversity in different parts of the world. These are lessons on Ubuntu, an African philosophy that translates into the words "I am because we are." Nelson Mandela emphasized this philosophy with a vision of an integrated, prosperous and peaceful South Africa and the world at large. Not only did he embody this concept, but also lived it. Ubuntu, "I am because we are," is a philosophy that describes the oneness of humanity, by sharing ourselves with others and caring for others.

I want to see a better understanding between cultures and ethnic backgrounds. I want to promote the spirit of "Ubuntu". It's the spirit of togetherness, that we are all connected and that we can all make a difference in the way things are. It is through this spirit that I have been able to realize my dream of becoming a Commonwealth Youth Forum Representative and in 2013, I had the extreme privilege to sit and interview his holiness the Dalai Lama.

I Have the Power

I Have The Power is the story of an African child, born in a remote area in Zambia: me. It follows the journey of my life with all the challenges of being born as a girl in a Southern African country. Mother Theresa said, "It's not how much we do, but how much love we put into the actions that we do." It's time to reflect on what it is we want for our communities, our homes and our personal legends. How do we contribute to our communities? How can YOU be of significance to YOUR community?

I joined the Rotary club when we first moved to Horsham a few years ago. I found that my values are very much aligned with that of Rotary. The charity work that we do as a collective is very inspiring and to know that we are creating significant change around the world makes me feel good. I love the works of the Rotary club and what we stand for.

This book is for you and is dedicated to all the young people out there.

Nkandu Beltz

Airborne exercise Tsau, Botswana, 2002

Chapter 1:

Born to be a Change-maker

> *"My mission in life is not merely to survive, but to thrive; and to do so with some passion, some compassion, some humour, and some style."*
>
> **Maya Angelou**

As I was my parents' firstborn child, they did whatever they could to ensure that I had a solid foundation for my future. When a couple gets a firstborn girl child, the messages of 'congratulations' come out like a death has just happened. Instead of congratulations, new parents who got a baby girl get "my condolences, it's a girl? I'm sure the next one will be a boy". So from the moment you take your first breath you are classified as a second-class citizen and that is what society has set you up for.

I Have the Power

But for my parents this was not the case. My dad would not allow me to be victimized because of my gender. I guess my grandparents had a huge influence on me as well. I was the youngest person in my grandparents household, surrounded by uncles and I would not take no for an answer nor lick anyone's boots. My father consolidated the belief of raising an outspoken girl child, but in my teenage years, he said he regretted this as he thought I might not get a husband and if I did, I would only last two days due to my outspoken nature and will not bend backwards for anyone.

My journey as a child was never smooth, but I had a pretty much 'normal' childhood, depending on what is classified as normal. I was admitted in hospital a few times, and was once poisoned in what was believed to be associated with witchcraft. What I remember is going to my friend's birthday party. I remember having a piece of cake that was specifically reserved for me. I don't recollect events after that or how I got home, but I remember finding myself in a hospital in Katete with my grandmother and mum on my bedside. I was told that Mum looked for me after the party, as the sun had set and it was way too dark for me to be outside. My parents thought I had gone to visit my grandmother's sister, Mrs. Mwanza, who lived a few kilometres from our house. I wasn't there, so Mum checked to see if I had taken any of my possessions with me before they went to the police station to report me as missing.

Mum found me lying on my bed and said I had swelled up like a balloon. She could see I was breathing, but non-responsive. They took me to the hospital immediately, where the diagnosis of 'poisoning' was made. Someone had inserted a poisonous substance into my vagina! It was a plant-based substance. The doctors at the Children's Hospital in Ndola could not do much and said that I was going to die. The poison had gone in my bloodstream and my kidneys were failing. I was diagnosed with Nephrotic

Chapter 1: Born to be a Change-maker

Syndrome, which might have been caused by acute kidney failure, thus explaining the swelling and rapid reaction. The doctor asked my mother to take me home and bring me back when things got really bad. Mothers are great and I thank God for mine; because she never gave up on me. My mother called my grandmother for advice and Grandma Edna Mnangagwa asked my mum Ethel to bring me to Katete immediately. You must be kidding, leaving the country's biggest children's hospital to go to Saint Francis' Hospital in Katete? My grandparents had heard of a Dutch doctor who was about to leave to go back to the Netherlands.

When we arrived in Katete, my parents went straight to this Dutchman's house and asked him to see me. He came over to the hospital, took one good look at me, and decided to stay a bit longer to help me out. I stayed in hospital for more than three months on diets that were so healthy, it sucked. I hated the food so much that even now, I hate the smell of hospitals and hospital food. Most of the food consisted of boiled or steamed chicken and carrots. This doctor saved my life; my parents acted very quickly and never gave up hope. If you know that a person has a chance of living through your actions, you have to do whatever you can to preserve a life and that is what this doctor did. I never had the chance to thank him personally, but I hope one day I get to meet my superhero again so that I can do so. No matter how bad the situation, you have to hope for the best until your last breath.

You would never think of turning a mother and daughter away from a hospital in Australia. However, I do not blame the medical industry in my birth country, as the system is pretty much screwed; the corruption has destroyed a country that could be one of the richest countries in Africa if it were governed properly.

The health and education systems have gone from bad to worse; I hold no anger or resentment towards what happened to me or the person trying to kill me. But these are just some of the challenges that I faced as a girl child, many African girls and girls in general around the world face even worse crimes during their lives. I guess this is one of the things that made me passionate about girl child rights. This is one of my first poems to rebel as a girl child.

> *"I may be their child by official marriage or correspondence,*
> *The surname is not enough for an identity,*
> *Maybe neighbours know the truth of what parents say about daughters and sons.*
> *Clothing, feeding, caring—all these are universal duties,*
> *Why a son more than a daughter?*
> *Here I stand, a young child I am*
> *Should I suffer because I was born in this Dark Continent?*
> *Or should I suffer because I was born a girl?*
> *I may be black or brown, but the soul is one and I need love and care*
> *A boy sitting in the sitting room while a girl working in the kitchen*
> *Is it really fair, my brothers and sisters?*
> *We need the right to express ourselves, the right to leadership capabilities, the right to medical facilities, to promote our future yes, promote our future.*
> *From childhood to teenage hood, you discouraged us from courageous jobs*
> *A boy, given a toy car and a girl given a doll*
> *Is it because I was born a girl?"*

Chapter 1: Born to be a Change-maker

I never liked dolls as a child; even now at 30, I still don't like them. Zambia is a very traditional country and it is also a Christian nation, but I personally find that the rules and traditions are set to oppress women and children. For example, I have to wear a chitenge in the presence of my father and any male person around me to avoid them seeing my legs and feminine curves. Even though the chitenge is just a piece of cotton, I find it oppressing and a way of intimidating women. It has nothing to do with respect or tradition; our ancestors wore minimal clothing. Some say it's to cover our legs so that men are not tempted to rape you, but I'm sure these men can control themselves.

If a man is sick in the head, no matter what you wear, he will still commit a crime. I think it's high time that people stopped oppressing women by dress code. I'm not saying let's go out in public without any clothes; what I'm saying is let women have a sense of self and dress appropriately. As a child, I was forced to keep my hair short, so most of the time I looked like a very cute boy; I was in pants except for Saturdays and school periods. On our way to church on Saturday mornings, I was wearing pants (without my parents' consent), which I folded up to my knees so that I could wear them immediately after church.

My churches in Zambia and Botswana would not allow you to wear shorts or pants. So, coming from a home where I would hear, "Nkandu, don't let anyone ever suppress your integrity or tell you what to do just because you are a girl!" and then going into the world where you are expected to shrink and bow down so that you won't stand out in front of boys and men was very confusing.

The girl child movement or the fight for equal rights has been going on for years. Recently, more than 200 girls were abducted in Nigeria. One of the reasons given was that they should not get a

I Have the Power

western education, but it's a way of supressing women! However, our African tradition regardless of religion, does not supress girls or women. Our ancestors had strong respect for women. We had strong female leaders and we still do. These are just some of the realities other girls face in some countries but despite all this, we still rise and lead in our own unique way.

The move to Botswana was one of the best things my parents did for us. I love Zambia with all my heart, but Botswana has a very special place in my heart. It's in Botswana that my sense of being was consolidated. I learned to look at things from a different perspective and to live my life without fear. I was in boarding school for the last two years of high school, and this was pure freedom for me. I loved boarding school and would do it again; I had a great time. I had great friends and teachers, and was finally in an environment that was relaxed. I could fit in and stand out. It was at Maun Senior Secondary School that I also learned to fully embrace my weirdness. It was during lunchtime that I was caught eating my sandwich.

I have a habit of eating peanut butter and jam together on a sandwich. One of my friends looked at me and said, "Nkandu! Are you going to eat that?" I said "Yes" with a smile. She looked at me with a face full of disgust and said, "You are weird." I looked at her, thought for a minute, and told her, "I love peanut butter and I love jam, so I just combine the two and eat it. Sweetie, weird is good; it's unique and different."

We have to embrace our weirdness and just love our differences. Imagine if we were all the same, everybody would like the same food and drinks; life would be so extremely boring. I have always been conscious about the food I eat. My mother had a veggie patch, so we ate straight from the earth. Growing up in Africa I knew where the meat came from and what the chooks ate. We had a

Chapter 1: Born to be a Change-maker

few cows on the farm, and after the cows had been milked, I often drank the milk straight from the containers without any treatment.

The first time I drank full cream milk in Australia, I was quite disappointed, as the taste was completely different from what I was used to — it tasted like it was diluted. It is not so much about the quality of the food product, but about the way the food is grown and how the people working on farms are treated. Healthy eating and environmental sustainability are very important. The lesser the distance the food has to travel, the better it is for you and the environment. We are encouraged to eat when we are hungry, stop when you are full and rest when we are tired. I found this concept hard to understand during my travels in developed nations. Children are encouraged to finish the food on their plates, as it is rude not to empty it. I think this may be one of the causes for obesity. People overeat and don't know when to stop. Then they spend money trying to lose those calories.

In Botswana, I learned about 'The Art of Living'. This was a teaching on healthy eating and training your body, mind and soul to live a balanced life. Have you ever wondered about were your food comes from? What is in your water and what chemicals are used to treat your fruit? Or should you simply leave it to someone else to do that job? Should you trust others to look after your health and wellbeing? One day, I was watching television—something that I don't do often and I was very shocked to learn about what had happened in Bangladesh. A total of 1,129 people died when the Rana Plaza Complex in Dhaka collapsed in April 2013.

This was one of the factory complexes that produced clothes for a range of western companies, including some Australian outlets. Six months later, another report stated that 94% had not received any legal benefits from their employers, while 92% reported being deeply traumatized, with over half experiencing insomnia and trembling from loud sounds. You can only imagine what the families of these workers are going through. At that moment, I wondered where my clothes came from. Who is making them and how are those human beings are treated?

As I did my research, I found that most clothes I was wearing came from China, but I could not track down the working conditions in the factories. I started sourcing ethically made clothes. I also included checking sources of my jewellery. I would ask where the gems were coming from and if the shopkeeper did not know, I would walk out. I do not want to support any business that has no idea where the products they are selling are coming from and how the workers making those products are being treated. Of course this reduces my chances of buying something nice, but I refuse to fuel modern-day slavery. One of the best ways to put an end to all this is by buying local products, supporting your local famers and buying from markets. I do not have all the answers, but you should all question what you eat, what you wear, where it's coming from and whether it is good for the environment.

I chose to be Nkandu when I was in the 8th grade. I was almost 13 and knew I had a talent; I was more confident than anyone else. I knew I could have a conversation with anyone and still be comfortable in my own skin. When I started high school, a lot of bullying went on around the school. I was very fortunate I never had a severe bullying incident in high school apart from girls spreading rumours that I was both anorexic and bulimic, as I was incredibly thin. After a month or two, I thought something was wrong with me, as I was not gaining any weight. I would eat sweet potatoes for breakfast and load up on sugar in my tea, but nothing happened. I would make fat cakes and eat them throughout the day. They don't call them fat cakes for nothing: these are an African version

Chapter 1: Born to be a Change-maker

of flapjacks, fried in cooking oil and loaded with sugar.

I went to ask my father if there was something wrong with me. Was the poisoning from my childhood affecting my body weight? Dad looked me in the eye and said, "You are perfect just the way you are." My father never said, "I love you," nor was he an affectionate kind of guy, but after those words, I stopped force-feeding on carbohydrates and started eating a healthy diet again.

It was at that point that I chose to follow my heart, to be happy with who I am, and to understand that people will always have something to talk about. I chose to wake up every morning and look in the mirror and smile. "You are created with a lot of potential, but to tap into this, you need to be able to love the face looking back at you in the mirror." Confidence and character are always together and you can never have character without confidence, as that would be disastrous.

One of the games I used to play was what many people call "fake it until you make it". Here is how it worked: if I found myself in a situation that I had no idea what to do with or how to respond, I would ask myself, "How would Oprah Winfrey react to this?" Based on what I thought Ms Winfrey would do, I would go ahead and do it. Never allow anyone to make you feel inferior; you are designed to grow, to blossom and to live an abundant life. But what builds character is your innermost thoughts.

Don't allow the world to put you in a box or tell you how to be. Every now and then, someone would remind me that I was a girl who belonged in the kitchen, but I refused to bend over backwards to accommodate such thinking. Just because you are born into a certain family, on a certain continent or in a certain cultural group does not mean you cannot rise to be the best you can be. People, including governments, want you to fit into a box. They will tell you to think outside the box, yet you cannot move outside that box. Yes, you can wiggle your hands and perhaps your feet, but at some point, they want you in that box.

Be who you want to be, ask for advice and get a good mentor. If you are not sure of who you want to be, that's ok; you still have enough time to figure it out. Look at people you admire; my heroes are everyday people, like doctors who save lives, police who keep us safe, my neighbour who looks out for me and the stranger who opened the door for me. All the people I meet are part of my journey. But you should not be defined by your sex, race, or educational background.

You have to make a choice about everything! We make a thousand choices every day: what to wear, when to wake up, what to eat for breakfast and what attitude we will give our friends. Sometimes we think we are just cruising through life, but the truth is, we are making choices. So why not make smart choices about who you want to be, what you want to be and the kind of friend you want to be?

I see a lot of good things happening in this world; I'm naturally an optimistic person. I see a world where young people no longer wait for permission to shine; they are the game changers in technology and social enterprise. They are emotionalizing education. I see classrooms as a way of the past. I think in the near future, social hubs will be mushrooming where young people with similar interests can meet and be educated by a skilled teacher in that field. When I started my campaign, we didn't have Facebook or Twitter. Social media has made it so easy to spread a message.

Chapter 1: Born to be a Change-maker

My friend Adorate when I was at Masala secondary school

You Have The Power

1. When you look at yourself in the mirror what do you think your purpose on Earth is?

   _____

   _____

   _____

2. Who is your favourite author and why?

   _____

   _____

   _____

3. What has been one of the toughest situations you have ever been in and how did you overcome it?

   _____

   _____

   _____

Chapter 2:
A Country Childhood

> "Some people succeed because they are destined, but most succeed because they are determined."
>
> **Henry Van Dyke**

I was born in a small country town called Katete, in the Eastern part of Zambia at Katete District Hospital. Katete is a small, vibrant town, full of colour and good people. Katete lies at the feet of Mpangwe and Kangarema Hills, close to the Katete River, which gives it a beautiful scenic view with its wildlife and the largest bird sanctuary in the country along the Luangwa Valley.

The women in Katete are always dressed in vibrant colours of African print material, commonly known as chitenges. These women would mostly be carrying babies on their backs on the way to the markets. These are not like the Queen Victorian markets in Melbourne; these are places where women have to work three times harder than men and have to bargain for deals.

Katete will always have a special place in my heart. I loved the traditional ceremonies. Long before the British introduced Christianity to the African countries, most Africans were worshiping a higher power through their ancestors, with seven days of dance, songs, food and acts of kindness. One of my favourite memories is that of 'Ncwala', the most important traditional festival of the Ngoni people. This is a ritual of thanksgiving to the God Almighty for the green. This happens after harvest, as most people in Zambia are subsistence farmers. It's very colourful and probably the most popular among Zambian traditional ceremonies. The people dress in leopard skins and carry things like knobkerries, shields and feathers. A bull is slaughtered and the paramount chief is served with its fresh blood to drink. The kill is then shared with the rest of the community.

Despite the poverty and hunger going around in the majority of homes, people still would congregate at public places to play African drums, women would be singing and children would play with whatever they could find. Most of the people I knew were from very poor families. I knew this because my uncle and I had to deliver food parcels that my grandparents had prepared.

My grandfather, Paul K. Mwale was a High Commissioner with the Community Development Association. He knew the families that were struggling and he and my grandmother, who was a school deputy headmaster, would pick vegetables from the garden, put them in a basket and hand it over to us to drop at certain houses. Sometimes there would be eggs, sometimes chooks or ducks, sometimes an animal kill that would be shared around.

Chapter 2: A Country Childhood

The sense of community in Katete had always fascinated me and as a child, I thought that was just normal. If your neighbour doesn't have food, you share what you have. My grandparents didn't have a lot, but they had a sense of community. Sometimes the community members would come and help us with our yard, with the harvest and even little things like cooking. My grandmother looked after many children; we called the house "open home" and sometimes I would wake up having no idea who would be at the breakfast table.

Most of the people who came to us were somehow related, but some were total strangers. Regardless, my grandmother would look after them until they found a place. The house was a large white, old-style European house with five bedrooms and a front veranda overlooking the hills. I learned to smile often and show gratitude. I learned from a young age to be genuinely interested in people. Not to just ask, "How are you?" The response you will get will be, "I'm fine thank you, and you?" Ask how the person is feeling. Connect with that person.

I always knew I was fortunate, as I did not go hungry and had all my needs met. I knew I was very lucky because we could afford to have proper meals and live in a very good house. Most of my friends were not so fortunate; some didn't even have the bare necessities. Some of my friends would come to school without shoes—but that was the least of their worries. The gap between the rich and the poor in most African countries, including Zambia, is massive. We have separate places for rich people, including shopping centres and churches, and we have markets with broken sewage pipes where most poor people will be buying their food. We have private hospitals and colleges opposite public ones, mostly with very limited or no funding, where children are dying every day from preventable illnesses. Sanitation is a big problem in most compounds, but if you walk 500 meters from that area, you will find yourself in posh suburbs with high electric-wall fences and lush green gardens with security guards at the front gate. I want you to take a moment to think about these huge differences and then reflect on your own life and count all the good things you have; we have so much to be grateful for.

> "When we seek to discover the best in others, we somehow bring out the best in ourselves."
>
> **William Arthur Ward**

Having spent quality time with my grandfather PK, I learned to feel deeply for others at a very young age. That does not mean I don't feel for myself. I knew I was very much loved and he spoilt me rotten. The traditional relationship with my grandfather was that I was equal to my grandmother, which gave me the same powers in the house. The traditional role for my grandmother was to be my legal guardian who had to protect me. However, I knew that I was not the centre of the universe; I knew from a very young age that I needed to contribute to making this world a better place. I suppose when you grow up in Africa, even though you are coming from a good home, you can see poverty immediately when you step out of your door. The people who worked on my grandparents' farms had nothing. Almost none of them had electricity or running water. Sometimes my grandparents would have to give their clothes to these families, especially in cold weather. We would go into our cupboards and select clothes to give away. My grandmother had

Chapter 2: A Country Childhood

one rule, "If it's not good enough for you, it's not good enough to give anyone!" She was right in every way. Why would you give clothes that are torn or so badly worn out that even you couldn't wear them?

You don't have to be rich to give: you can give smiles; you can use your skills to help others; you can give books which are one of my favourite treasures; you can give clothes to charities and sports equipment to clubs or you can donate money to a cause that is aligned to your values. Ask your friends and family, instead of getting you a whole heap of presents that will end up in the bin one week after your birthday, to instead support a charity that deals directly with poor people. Imagine waking up in the morning, having no idea what you will eat, and having to walk a long distance to get food that could potentially kill you because of possible contamination.

It was only natural for me to do what I do. To be of service to my country and any community I live in. We have a greeting in Africa that says, "Nabajyotisaika" which means "I respect you, I cherish you, you matter to me," and the other person responds with "Shokoba" which translates into "I exist for you." Once you get to realise that we are all connected and we are all an embodiment of everything that we see, you can never do anything for the benefit of yourself but for others, and this is done through the concept of Ubuntu. I don't think I could do anything else.

Everything I want to do has to benefit others. I always ask myself this in the morning, "How can I be of great service to those around me?" There is a difference between servitude and being a servant. The service I offer comes from my heart, it's genuine and I enjoy giving. I was really moved by the many little acts of kindness my grandparents offered to those around us. These little acts of

I Have the Power

kindness have shaped me into the woman I am today. I feel like if I died today, I would tell God that I did my best for him and mankind. Every morning, I practise gratitude. I go through everything that I'm grateful for in my life and when I say everything, I mean *everything*, including the clean air I breathe, the warm shower I take in the morning, the food on the table and the gift of life and health.

When I was 17, my best friend Jane Opperman and I would take 15% of our allowance to buy fruit and toys for poor people who were admitted at the hospital. In most African public hospitals, the food is pretty bad and not nutritional at all. So for those that can afford a good hospital bed, they would get a good meal and for the poor, they have to do with what they have or get from visiting family. This little act of kindness that I learnt from my grandparents made me a happy person, and Jane and I would always leave the hospital feeling good about ourselves. The feeling was so great because we made someone smile, we made someone realise that people actually do care about others. I'm the woman who would organise an event to help people I have never met; I'm the woman who will go out of her way to help a friend because I can and because if I needed help, you would do the same. We are all lovers of humanity and no matter how small the acts of kindness, they go a long way.

As an important member of your community, everything you do has an impact, either on you or those around you. "However small they may seem, your decisions have an impact on the quality of your life and the relationships with other people." Whatever you do or say can either make someone happy or break them down. Your actions speak the loudest. No act of kindness is ever wasted. One thing that I have learned through this journey of who I am and who I want to be is that sometimes your best is not good enough; you will find people who will just want to take and not give back. Despite this, you should stay true to yourself and follow your gut feeling.

Chapter 2: A Country Childhood

My childhood helped me to build a solid foundation and to create a woman who believes in herself. I had the privilege of learning and knowing about my roots; of what my people before me did and the care they gave. I am a woman who can never be broken, only bent. I know I can change the world! Change starts with me; it starts inside of me. I started realizing that I could make a difference when I initiated my public performances. When I spoke, people listened and acted. They wanted to help. I always believed I was born to make a difference.

The realization of who I am as a person did not happen overnight, and sometimes I still ask myself "Who am I?" But one thing I know is that I'm a significant human being who is part of an awesome team called the human race. I know for sure that if you surround yourself with people you admire, people who add value to your life and people who are interested in your development as a person, you will move to higher grounds. Never settle for mediocrity. My mother had a massive influence in my life; I guess she knew that the kind of clothes I was wearing would determine the way I behaved. For example, as a child playing in a jungle gym, wearing combat pants and black T-shirts, the boy in me would come out. But my mother would also make some beautiful elegant dresses that my sister and I would wear. Those were the times I would behave like a lady. I enjoyed the dresses; I loved the way I felt wearing them. Even now, as a grown woman, I have my power shoes and power dresses, and when I'm on stage wearing them, it feels like having a talisman with me. I'm not sure if it's more about the clothes or more about the girl staring back at me in the mirror.

I Have the Power

Women doing a traditional Zambian dance

Chapter 2: A Country Childhood

African women at the market

Traditional dance ceremony

I Have the Power

Victoria Falls

Chapter 2: A Country Childhood

You Have The Power

1. What causes do you care about most?

_____

_____

_____

_____

_____

2. What would it take for you to lend your voice to this particular cause?

_____

_____

_____

_____

_____

3. How would it make you feel having accomplished your mission?

_____

_____

_____

_____

_____

Chapter 3:

From a Land of Kings and Queens

> "You are capable of making a difference in the way things are by making decisions responsibly and carefully based on the facts you gather."
>
> **Unknown**

The first time I met Dr. Kenneth Kaunda still seems like a dream. I was wearing brown pants again; this was a sign of me being comfortable in my own skin. My grandmother had insisted I wear a dress as a sign of respect, as every girl giving flowers to the president must wear a dress or something feminine. This was a battle I had most of my childhood and even now, as a grown woman, I still have disagreements with my parents as to what a woman should wear.

I Have the Power

My grandfather was happy for me to wear my brown pants and the light blue blouse that my grandmother had brought me from Zimbabwe. My grandmother is from Zimbabwe and her family still lives in Harare and other remote areas. I also wore my coloured bangles, which I loved dearly. I had seven of them with colours of the rainbow and my hair was braided in cornrows with white, yellow and red beads in them.

I remember as a child I wanted to be as important as the man I saw walking towards me. He was tall, and wearing a dark grey suit, but the one thing that fascinated me the most was the white handkerchief in his hand. I assumed it was his talisman. He waved his hand with his white handkerchief as he stepped out of the plane. He walked towards us and I gave him the flowers. I had to bend my knees, as it is custom to do so when handing something to someone older than you. He was just like my grandfather: warm-hearted; calm and full of love. I could tell it was a happy visit.

That afternoon, we had lunch at the community development commission offices. The dining room was full of important people wearing suits and I was the only child—a girl for that matter—and wearing pants! The adults seemed to ignore me. I sat quietly eating my food, talked only when I was spoken to, and smiled when someone looked at me. I had no idea what the meeting was about, but the men and women in the room were very civilized.

Dr. Kenneth Kaunda, or "Dr. KK", as we call him, is the founding father of our nation, Zambia. He and his 'freedom fighter' friends fought for independence and I hear our country shed so much blood that they decided to put the colour red on the national flag as a reminder of the lives we lost during the struggle. Zambia was a British protectorate and we gained independence in 1964. We often joke in my family that the best thing the British left for us was the tradition of afternoon tea with scones and jam.

Chapter 3: From a Land of Kings and Queens

Dr. KK stood for solidarity; he always encouraged people to walk as one. He came up with the slogan of 'One Zambia, One Nation', in the hope that all the ethnic groups in the country could be united. Most people don't know that Zambia has 72 languages, and over 50 different tribes. The country is divided into 10 provinces and all the tribes are unique with different traditions. I guess what impressed me most about Dr. KK was his ability to mix with the poor as well as the rich.

Dr. KK shook hands with poor people and listened to them, then did the same with the rich people. I thought that if such a man could walk with kings, talk with commoners and still keep his virtue, then I want to grow up to be just like him. I had heard of how he had helped Nelson Mandela, how he stood on a podium with Martin Luther King and shook hands with Queen Elizabeth.

I remember looking up to powerful African female leaders and I still do. Dr. Kenneth Kaunda's wife Betty was one remarkable lady, caring for orphans and the poorest families in our country; Maureen Nkandu as woman in Media, News Anchor and fighter for social justice; my Aunty Christabelle Nyawengo, the first female engineer to work for Zambian Airlines; and Graca Machel, politician, humanitarian and international advocate for women's and children's rights. But as an African child, my grandfather told me stories about the history of our land with female heroes long before these present-day heroes.

My grandfather told me about the importance of knowing your past. I come from a land of Queens and Kings! My top five favourite powerful African Queens are Queen Cleopatra, Queen Tiye, the Nubian Queen of Egypt, Queen Amina from Ghana, Queen Nandi, Shaka Zulu's mother and my favourite of all time, Queen Nzingha from Angola. These women were powerful, courageous and they truly cared for their people. They were selfless and sacrificed a lot for their people. Some of them were active military leaders (e.g.,

I Have the Power

Queen Nzingha, who formed an alliance with the Dutch to fight against the Portuguese).

My father said I was named after his aunty Nkandu, who was one of the most powerful female leaders in his village. The word 'Nkandu' means 'the Generous One', and my middle name, 'Makili', means 'the Happy One'. "What's in a name?" one might say. However, most of my leadership is influenced not only from what I seem to be, but what I read as well. As a lover of books, I would go towards poetry most of the time. I still love collecting quotes from people who inspire me. Here are some quotes that I have kept for a very long time.

> "You are someone with special talents to share with others."

> "Take the time to learn what your talents are, then use them to make this world a better place for everyone."

Of all the stories and books I have read, I've been inspired by these people and felt powerful enough to go and make a difference in the world.

Chapter 3: From a Land of Kings and Queens

Most people who have been victims of domestic violence or rape will tell you that when someone forces him or herself on you can be one of the most intimidating things in life. It's about power and dominance. Nothing had prepared me for what happened in my headmaster's office. This was a man of authority, who was paid to teach and protect me. When I was in high school, my headmaster sexually abused me. I was 15 years old. I was called to go and see him. His secretary looked at me in a strange way. I thought I was in trouble but did not care that much. I was a social butterfly and it was not unusual for people to seek my presence. My parents had moved to Botswana and I was staying with my aunty. He asked me to close the door behind me. He was a very dark man, very black-skinned and scary looking. Rumours had it that he had sold his soul to the devil. He sat in his chair while I stood in his office; and asked me if I had been to a hotel before. I said yes; my father often took us to hotels to have breakfast as a treat.

He asked if I knew where the Savoy Hotel was in the city. He said I could meet him there. He then stood up and came close to me, then took my hand and put it on his penis. I was frozen; he then started to kiss me. It was my first kiss. I was in shock; I had no idea what to do. It was the most disgusting thing that had ever happened to me. I immediately asked him to move back and I threatened to scream. He held me closer and I raised my voice, shouting for him to let go of me. At that moment, his secretary knocked on the door, asking if everything was ok. She saved my life! I ran out of the office, straight to the toilets and washed my hands, face and mouth. I sat outside the classroom for the entire period. I was then late for science class and my science teacher thought it would be good to punish me for coming late and not answering her questions. She then made me kneel down the entire science period. I was in tears the whole time.

I Have the Power

When I shared the story with two of my best friends, they both said I should never say a word, as I would be in so much trouble. A girl never speaks about such things. So the assault was never reported and I now regret not telling anybody. I have found that the system was designed to make us fail. Had I known I had the power over this man, I would have reported the case to my Aunty and more cases would probably have come out which would have led to his arrest. The reason why girls are vigorously told NOT to report is the fact that when the perpetrator is convicted and sent to prison, his family would be without finances and would possibly go hungry!

Despite all this, I did not lose faith in mankind. I was just more vigilant and careful around grown-ass shit men with dirty minds. Anyone who has gone through this kind of situation or worse should know that there is support available around them. You are not a victim, no matter how bad the situation; you can rise above it, seek help, and choose to live and be a phenomenal being. It was not easy, but I have risen above it all and that experience has taught me to be extra kind; I never want to inflict such pain on anyone. If you want something badly enough, the universe opens up the doors for you to get what you want. As I got older, I desperately needed to have a coach in public speaking; my father and my English teacher were not enough.

When I was about 13 years old, the Drama Club was doing auditions for a play. Owas Ray Mwape was directing the production. He was an accomplished actor and had made a name for himself. He was on television most of the time and was doing very well. My geography teacher asked me to go to the school hall and give it a go. As I stepped into the hall, I saw Mr. Mwape at the back of the hall as students one by one did their magic. He asked me what I wanted; I told him I wanted to join his club. He asked if I could act; I said no, but that I could learn. He asked me to get on stage and show him

Chapter 3: From a Land of Kings and Queens

what I had. I recited the girl child poem. He stopped me halfway through the recital and asked me to use a stronger voice and to move less. I had to look at the audience and slow down as I spoke. I did just that. He looked at me, smiled, and said, "See you at the rehearsals."

Owas was and still is a very handsome man. He took me under his wing and helped me spread the message about girl child rights and equality from that time onward. He wrote all the poems, directed them and taught me how to speak and make an impact. It was like he found his female voice. I was an instrument that he could use and I was very happy that finally someone of great calibre could work with me and direct me. I spoke at school assemblies, at all the drama competition events, at the Mulugnushi International Conference Centre in Lusaka and at Independence Day celebrations. We travelled around the country and won lots of poetry and drama competitions on a national level.

Owas was not a man to only raise awareness on the injustice of the girl child, but he also talked about HIV and AIDS. He wrote poems that I would recite about the cruel disease killing my people. He wrote plays that I would act in. Most of the time, I was the girl who introduced the production. I was the face of the Drama Club, and I loved it.

In 1994, when the genocide happened in Rwanda, I was 11. I was going about my day-to-day life when the news broke. I was not so much affected by it until a few years later when Owas wrote a poem about being a refugee. He gave me the script to memorize and his words still echo in my head. He said, "Nkandu, that's your part. You are a refugee from Rwanda, seeking food and shelter." As I read the script, tears ran down my cheeks. My words were few but like they say, a picture tells a thousand words.

I Have the Power

The day of the competition came. I wore my black and white dress, which my mother had torn to pieces; it was soaked in red ink to make it look like blood. I had a small bundle of clothing with me at my side. I walked on stage slowly, after all the other Drama Club members had said their parts, looking down at the ground, crying. I was barefoot and dusty. I did not eat the day before and I did not eat breakfast that morning. As I spoke with my loud, strong, confident voice, I said:

> *"People look at me,*
> *you may think that I have been saved from a lion's mouth,*
> *but that's not true.*
> *I have come here in fear of my life.*
> *Right now, I'm just trespassing on your land.*
> *My mother and father, brothers and sisters have all been killed by our neighbour.*
> *What shall I do?*
> *Where shall I go?*
> *I need food and shelter.*
> *Please help me."*

After the last words, I broke down and cried on stage. We won the competition and the judges cried with me. The audience cried with me. Everyone could relate and understand what had been happening in Rwanda. Zambia had so many refugees and we needed to help them more. This was not an act; this was due to the realization of how lucky I was to have a mother and father; how lucky I was to live in a peaceful country.

Chapter 3: From a Land of Kings and Queens

The breaking point was the realization that a 10-year-old girl had lost her entire family due to a tribal war and was all alone in this world, looking for food and shelter. This was the realization that the refugee girl, the girl without shoes or a spare change of clothes, could be me. The Owas Ray Mwape productions did not only open my eyes to what was happening on the African continent, but taught me to speak on behalf of the oppressed. I can't lie and say I walked in their shoes, but in Africa, we have a saying, "Only the pot knows how hot the fire is." What I can say is that I was given a platform on which to express myself, to share the message and to do what I loved and still love doing: standing in front of people.

At that stage in life, communication and raising awareness through drama was the only tool I had. I made use of it. You can make a difference at any age. You don't have to wait to be a grown-up to help other people. The difference that you can make exists around you today. Take a moment to look around you. I was 10 when I found out I could use my voice! We had no Facebook, Twitter or Snapchat! It was not easy to get the message out to thousands of people, but today it's with the touch of a button.

As Ghandi said, "Be the change you want to see in the world." You are the agents of change; you have a lot of power and potential to make a difference. Talk to your friends; find out what they care about. Come up with solutions and ask people to help. Someone is always there to help. You are never alone.

I Have the Power

Chapter 3: From a Land of Kings and Queens

You Have The Power

1. How can you incorporate what you do in helping others without giving up your personal freedom and still have a good time?

_____

_____

_____

_____

2. What would you do if you found yourself in a similar situation like mine when I was 15?

_____

_____

_____

_____

_____

3. What services are in place nearby that could help you if you called them?

_____

_____

_____

_____

_____

Chapter 4:

Drastic Confrontations

> "Our dead are never dead to us, until we have forgotten them."
>
> **George Eliot**

Death is part of life. We should never be afraid of dying, but when we lose a loved one, the emptiness in our hearts is so massive; we feel that it will never be filled. The truth is, it will never be filled. However, once we accept that this is life, and life is about living, creating our existence and finding our passion, that's when we have lived, my friend. Life is for living! Take the time to fill it with love and beautiful moments. Create classic time, which will live forever. I had friends who were orphans and I had heard of people dying, but for myself, I had no close connection or experience with losing someone close to me or someone I knew. When my parents moved to Mongu in the western part of Zambia, I knew this place would be different.

I Have the Power

I loved my new neighbourhood; I loved my school and my new friends. I even found that the library was not far from home, which meant I could borrow books and return them anytime. My father was working for the Credit Union Saving Association of Zambia (CUSA-Zambia). Their aim was to provide services to locals such as agriculture loans, accounting and marketing for all credit unions in the country. The World Bank through CUSA supported a program to help farmers grow and sell their produce in the North Western Province of Zambia. My father was an auditor at that time. We had a company house and a company car. Our house had three bedrooms, a living room and a bathroom with a big backyard with a few cashew trees. We had better living conditions than most people. It was a good home and the environment was great.

Our new neighbourhood was expanding and the construction was done carelessly. One afternoon after school, a truck was digging sand and piling it up on the other side of the compound. In no time, a group of kids had gathered around and were rolling on this artificial hill as it kept getting bigger and bigger. For some reason, I sat in our yard, just watching what was going on. I felt these kids were brave: when the truck would bring the sand, the kids would roll down with the sand—until we heard a shrieking sound. One of the kids was crying that his friend had been buried. The truck driver stopped and began digging with his hands. A few more people came and started digging, too. I just sat there, watching all of this unfold.

Somehow, the driver was asked to use the truck to remove more sand from the pile. As he did this, he got too close to the boy. When he removed the layer of sand, he had scraped half of the boy's body! Blood and guts were all over the place! Someone got a blanket and covered the body. That was the closest I have ever gotten to death. I saw kids and women crying, shouting and screaming and the whole operation was stopped.

Chapter 4: Drastic Confrontations

I stood outside my house as the kids walked by and asked if they were ok. I knew I had to do something, but didn't know what to do. I offered to sit down and just listen to them as they shared their stories and they mentioned how they shouldn't have rolled down on the sand. Mind you, we had no 'counselling services' after this tragic incident. I sat under the cashew tree, talking to my friends and telling them it was not their fault; that God had decided that he wanted this boy back in heaven. For a week, we talked, sang songs and talked about all the funny jokes this boy liked to make. I found that in this time of tragedy, I had made some new friends. I had a listening ear and I thought I could do more in life.

> *"Make every day count, even when you think it's the worst day of your life, for you never know when it will be your last."*
>
> **Solange Nicole**

It was at that stage that I realized life was precious, that in an instant everything could change. I began by looking around me and appreciating everything in my life. I wanted to live a life so full that if I died, I would say to God, "I did my best, I rocked that earth and I lived it my way." But this lesson also meant that I became clingy to my loved ones. I would give long hugs to my parents. My dad was never an affectionate man, but I would give him hugs and tell him I loved him; I would thank my mother tirelessly for her cooking, cleaning and making our clothes. I would spend time with my siblings. All I wanted was to create memories that were so

I Have the Power

wonderful that if I died, they would only have good things to say about me. They would smile and say, "If she was here, we would be laughing about nothing at all."

A few months after that incident, one of my cousins came to visit us. My father did not know she had an underlying illness. One day, when my mother had gone to the market with her friend to buy food for the evening meal and my father was at work, she fell onto the floor and went into a fit. She was rolling around on the floor kicking her legs and arms in the air; I had no idea what to do. She was older than me and I was scared. I asked my sister to call my father at work to come quickly and asked my brother who was only seven years old, to go after mum. He found her only a few meters from home, coming back from the market.

She came running. I tried to move the table and chairs that my cousin had kicked; by this time, she was lying flat on the floor with her mouth full of white foam. My mother asked me to take the kids to the bedroom and she began performing first aid. A few minutes later, my father arrived. They put her in the back of the car and drove straight to the hospital as it was faster than calling an ambulance. After a few hours, mum came back with my father, both crying. We knew it was bad news. I was told that she had choked on her own saliva. My mother tried everything she could do, but she could not revive the girl.

When her family arrived in Mongu, they put the blame onto my father. Her mother talked about how my father would use her for witchcraft. My mother was heartbroken. My father thought it was a bad idea to have people over for holidays. I sat in my parents' bedroom with my siblings during the four days of mourning. We made little noise. We saw my parents crying as my cousin's parents blamed my parents. I felt that I had to do something. I spoke up that

Chapter 4: Drastic Confrontations

evening and told them how my mother ran towards the house, how she fell on the ground near their daughter, turning her on the side to drain the foam from her mouth and how she was the one who started performing CPR.

I told them that she is gone and never coming back. I could feel my father's strong hands holding me as I spoke, trying so hard to stop me from speaking. My parents just kept quiet as they were being blamed for something they had no control over. But I couldn't stand it; I could not keep quiet and just watch as the injustice was done. After the funeral, the family left and went back to Mansa. I thought my parents would never look after other people's children again, but a month later, another cousin arrived. My cousin had lost his father, so my father became his guardian and he would now live with us.

At these moments, I realized that no matter how hard and heartbreaking life can be, people do bounce back and will still care for others. The love and compassion my parents showed in caring for others made me realize how selfless humans can be. Life is precious. You don't have to experience tragedy to appreciate what you have. Live your life, love yourself and those around you and make sure you inspire others along the way.

Zambia is the largest copper export and yet one of the poorest countries in the world. Zambia is very rich in its natural resources and home to one of the Seven Wonders of the World, Mosi-O-Tunya (Smoke That Thunders), commonly known as the Victoria Falls. I spent a significant amount of time with my grandparents at their house overlooking the Katete River and the Mpangwe Hills before they moved to Nyimba.

I later joined my parents in Ndola, the capital of the Copperbelt, and started school at Masala Primary. It was there that I realised that a public life was calling. It was around this time that I realised how much injustice my birth country had towards the girl child. My family was neither wealthy nor poor. My parents had good jobs, we went to fairly good schools and we had enough to eat and to give to others.

It was in Ndola that I found out first-hand about the injustice towards girls; girls being treated like second-class citizens. It was in Ndola where I was encouraged to sit at the back of the class so that boys can have front-row seats. It was in Ndola where I learned that as a girl child, I shouldn't be wearing pants and I should have my hair very short like a boy so that I don't show off my feminine side as I might become a victim of rape. It was in this very city that my mother made my uniforms extra-long so that I wouldn't attract attention from the opposite sex by showing off my legs! But this very city, the heart of the Copperbelt, gave birth to a girl child advocate, a disruptor who would question and challenge the status quo. It was this very town that gave me the strength and courage to stand up and speak. It was this very town that supported me to be the girl child advocate.

My parents left for Botswana, but I stayed in Zambia until I was 15. I joined my parents in Maun, Botswana during my last two years of secondary education. Maun is the biggest village in Botswana, sitting at the edge of the Okavango Delta, the only inland delta in the world. It's a true man's paradise, with an abundance of wildlife and people. Maun was another stepping-stone. It provided me with a beautiful platform to contribute more to my community and I must confess, I had the best time in high school.

In Maun, while I was at Maun Senior Secondary School, I was a peer educator, counselling fellow students who were most troubled. That's when I joined the Botswana National Youth Council. As my

Chapter 4: Drastic Confrontations

other passion is writing, I would contribute poetry to the school newsletter and recite poems on stage during most school assemblies. I would also be invited to speak at parties and public forums on issues that affect young people.

My life took a turn into journalism and news writing. I thought it would be through news writing and reporting that I could help people and bring a voice to the voiceless. I went to the house where the Ngami Times, the local newspaper, was made and applied for a job as journalist. Norman Chandler, the owner, wasn't around, but his daughter, Tracey, gave me the job. After three months, I joined the Media Institute of Southern Africa.

Being part of the team at Ngami Times was great; I felt a sense of pride in writing for a newspaper. I would walk around with a notepad, pen and camera for anyone to see. However, this also put me right in the centre of reality for most people. I was a junior reporter and was mostly spending my time in court, at the police station, or seated under a tree while talking with victims and criminals. I reported on cases of rape, which then directed me to organisations like 'Women Against Rape'.

This reminded me of how lucky I was that my headmaster had not succeeded at raping me—some of these women had acquired HIV/AIDS. Some people I spoke with had been bank robbers, or rather, were accused bank robbers. There was so much sadness doing this job, I would occasionally write some good news stories, but like everyone will tell you, "bad news sells." The reality sank in, and more than 50% of women at that time had gone through some form of violence. I'm sure these statistics would be the same in many countries around the world.

I had to find an outlet. I love fashion and being 166cm tall does not qualify me to be an international model, but I could still model for local fashion designs. The money I raised through modelling would go straight towards helping people living with HIV/AIDS, or I could buy food and hand it out at the hospital. I had no time for self-pity, as I had so many around me in worse situations. The last fashion show I participated in was the Botswana Fashion week in 2002. It was a great experience and the ladies at the Botswana Council of Women had worked so hard to make sure that my friends and I were well looked after. Daisy Botsoba was our patron from Maun; she was really a great mentor to us. She has now opened up her own orphanage, as the number of kids on the streets keeps on rising.

Chapter 4: Drastic Confrontations

You Have The Power

1. What has been some of the confronting things you have come across in your life?

   _____

   _____

   _____

   _____

   _____

2. How did you resolve the issue or challenges? How did you use your power?

   _____

   _____

   _____

   _____

   _____

3. What have you learned from the situation? How has it made you stronger?

   _____

   _____

   _____

   _____

Chapter 5:

Becoming a Peer Educator

> *"There will never be complete equality until women themselves help to make and elect lawmakers."*
>
> **Susan B. Anthony**

I always knew that if I wanted to make a difference in people's lives, I had to be sure of who I was as a person and what I wanted from life myself. My life felt like a journey of self-discovery, a journey of who I was and who I wanted to be, but in all that, I would compromise as to what people wanted to see; I wanted to please everyone by being the person they thought I was. I began keeping a diary. I would write in my 'dear diary' every night before going to bed. By doing so, I found common patterns and trends. I wrote about the people I met, the conversations I had, the beauty of the sunset and how the tap water tasted so good. I realized that my life was full of gratitude, but at the same time I was so afraid to fail. I was afraid of saying 'no' to tasks, even though I knew I didn't have enough time to follow them through to completion.

When I finally found myself and fell in love with Nkandu Makili, I was confident enough to say 'no' to things that I did not have time for. I would wake up in the morning and look in the mirror and smile. I would remind myself that God took his time to create me. I'm a woman. I'm a wonderful woman and I only have to do what is right for me and for those around me.

> "The purpose of life is not to be happy. It is to be useful, to be honourable, to be compassionate, to ensure it makes some difference that you have lived and lived well."
>
> **Ralph Waldo Emerson**

When I started school at Maun Senior Secondary in Botswana, I was not very happy about the changes of living in a new country and starting all over again. In a land where no one knew me, I missed being called the girl child and being a mini-celebrity. My father's decision to live in Botswana was not a very welcoming concept, but he confiscated my passport and said that at 15 years of age, I was *his* child and he could choose where he wanted me to live and which school I should go to.

Chapter 5: Becoming a Peer Educator

My father told me I could make a difference anywhere in the world; he said I should listen to my heart and talk to the people around me, as someone will always need help. He said, "In any community you live in, seek to do good there, then when your services and skills are no longer needed, you can move to help in another community." My father was right. My first day of school was fun; I had been introduced to Stacy-Ann Medley a month before, my Jamaican friend with a very positive attitude. Stacy-Ann was very talkative and fun. I was also introduced to Rafael Mangra (a.k.a. "Mambo") and Jean Pierre Chinye, who became very good friends of mine.

The first day at school, I wanted to join the drama club, but the problem was the drama was all done in Setswana and as a new migrant, I did not speak the language, which turned out to be a massive challenge. I then told the teacher to give me three months and I would be back. Who learns a language in three months?

We had very good teachers; the school was international with most teachers and students coming from different parts of the world. I joined the PACT Club (Peer Approach to Counselling by Teenagers). Our patron was Mr. Murapedi, who was the guidance and counselling teacher. The first things we learned were basic psychology: how to tell when someone is distressed; looking for the warning signs and not getting attached to other people's problems. The problems Botswana was facing were huge: with a population of 1.5 million people, the HIV/AIDS infection rate was the highest in the world.

PACT was a program that strived to empower teens/adolescents (both male and female) to make personal informed decisions about important issues in their lives. PACT Club is still a youth-led club designed to provide and encourage safe, structured, supervised and frequent opportunities for teens to gain and share information with their peers, parents and other adults through workshops, seminars and other informational venues. The main goal of the club was to reach youth and other community members in remote areas to educate them about healthy living and give them a strong foundation in Life Skills.

That was through information sharing about HIV/AIDS prevention, nutrition, thoughtful decision-making, risk reduction, how to deal with peer pressure, health and hygiene. We also covered topics of life skills such as self-respect, love, gender equality, stigma and discrimination, gender-based violence, self-awareness, sex and appropriate dating techniques. Life Skills addressed the roots of behaviour that HAD TO change before the fight against HIV/AIDS could be won. The idea was to empower young people and give them self-confidence to make informed decisions. Our goal was not only to teach the youth about the dangers of HIV/AIDS, but also to model an individualized, interactive exploration of the meaning of human rights.

> "Everybody can be great...because anybody can serve. You don't have to have a college degree to serve. You don't have to make your subject and verb agree to serve. You only need a heart full of grace. A soul generated by love."
>
> **Martin Luther King, Jr.**

Chapter 5: Becoming a Peer Educator

During this time, I learned a lot about myself as well. I found that what most teens need was to feel accepted and to be loved. They wanted people to be nice to them and the bullying, the bitchiness and the 'acting cool' was just superficial, but deep down, how we treat others and how we make them feel is extremely important.

One day, after class had finished, I was walking back to the hostels and by then, I had become a boarder at Maun Senior Secondary School, a period I would recall as one of the best times of my life.

A girl called Mandy informed me that she had been gang-raped by her neighbours; the guys were very violent and the case had been reported to the police and was under investigation. What Mandy was afraid of more than going to court and being exposed, was having contracted HIV/AIDS. When the incident had occurred, her grandmother had taken her to the hospital and Mandy was given prophylactic medication to try to prevent the virus from infecting her body.

Mandy was one of the most intelligent girls in the school; very well-behaved and beautiful. The neighbours had blamed her for wearing clothes that were exposing her femininity. She asked me if I would go to court with her and just sit with her as the case went on. This happened toward the end of the year as we were preparing for our final exams. I did that; not because I was a peer educator, but because I knew she needed someone to be with her and not judge her. I found myself crying most nights, as I could feel her pain. During our training, we are taught not to become emotionally attached to our peers when it comes to dealing with such issues, but I must say, when a 16-year-old shares a personal story and you can see the pain in her eyes, you *will* get emotionally attached. I spoke with the Guidance and Counselling teacher and he contacted a women's lobby group, 'Women Against Rape'. A tough lady, who

I Have the Power

was very vocal when it came to the victimizing of women and children, headed this group and she wanted tougher punishments for the perpetrators.

It was in times like these that I knew these women would fight until the law was changed. It took four months for these guys to be convicted and during that time, I had started freelancing for the Ngami Times. I splashed the story in the newspaper during the trial and that turned out to be a very big mistake. Once the publication had gone to print, two guys followed me home, grabbed me by my neck and threatened to kill me. One of them had a knife and warned me never to write anything about them again. While all the drama was happening, my mobile phone, which I had gotten as a gift, rang. It was my Canadian friend, but I pretended to be talking to the detective superintendent, Mr. Kame, and answered with, "Yes they are here, I should have listened to you! They are right here and one of them has a knife, Mr. Kame!" The guys knew Mr. Kame, as he was one of the most respected policemen in Maun, a senior superintendent.

The boys pushed me to the ground and insulted me as they walked away. On the other end of the line, my friend was asking me, "What the hell was that? What is going on? Should I call the police?" *That was a close call*, I thought. I thanked him for saving my life and calling at that time, but I had to call the police. I rushed home, the police came straight over, and they asked if I wanted to file an incident report. I said no, as they would be going to jail anyway, but that was clearly a lesson learned. I thought I could help people through journalism by exposing what was happening in the community, but that was way too dangerous. Journalism is an excellent profession, and I know I'll go back to it one day, just not yet. I have tremendous respect for journalists and what they go through to get the news to us. It's not an easy job, but it's highly rewarding.

Chapter 5: Becoming a Peer Educator

Maun was a small town with a population of about 15,000 people. The town had some very good people; it was a typical Botswana village with goats and donkeys walking the street. The houses are all built in different directions. Sometimes you would find a beautiful house next to a traditional mud house. It was the Botswana (and many more African countries) way of life; they are very giving and love to celebrate. Sometimes we would find ourselves having a party for no reason. You start some loud music; someone will drop by with some meat and there you go—meat is roasting, the braai is going on and the crowd begins to grow. They are a very social and diverse group of people.

My love for social change-making was only natural. When so many people surround you, you see the gap between the rich and the poor. You see street kids without appropriate clothing, yet when you walk around the block, you see mansions and malls. But remember, you don't have to live in Botswana or Zambia to be able to do something good. Start where you are; look around you. The best way to start doing some good is by being kind to others. You never know when someone might just need that hug or your kind words. You might just be the difference in pulling someone back from the edge.

During my teenage years, I spoke with many of my peers about issues affecting them, from domestic violence to youth empowerment, and also to young people who wanted to be self-reliant and set up their own social enterprise ventures. When I finished school, I joined the Botswana National Youth Council (BNYC), another very cool organization that dedicates its services to helping young people in Botswana.

The structure of BNYC was very simple: we were a youth councils representing one of the 51 districts. It was the highest decision-making body on youth-related issues, and we had youth representatives in

I Have the Power

the National Assembly, which convened every twelve months. The main aim was to facilitate and implement youth activities, lobby and advocate for policy development, and give advice to government on matters that relate to youth. This meant that I had to travel to remote areas of Botswana, listen to young people, then record and write the concerns of my peers.

One of my most memorable trips was when I was asked to go the Gudikwa, a very remote area about 100km down a deep sandy road from Shakawe at the edge of Namibia along the Okavango River. The place was very hard to access. A lot of accidents happened along the way, on the sandy road or on the water, as the ferry you had to take to cross the Okavango River was not stable, and a few months before I travelled this way, it had capsized, killing five people who were trapped under the boat. We started off from Maun with Mr.Claude Gabanakemo and Jane Opperman. We had several stops along the way at Toteng, Sehitwa, Tsau, Nokaneng and Gumare. We then drove straight to Shakawe before crossing the Okavango River towards Seronga and Gadikwa. These places were as remote as you can get in Botswana, and most of the time, there was no running water or electricity. The travel by 4-wheel drive was a challenge in itself, and travelling during the rainy season was as good as impossible! But like they say, "When in Rome, do as the Romans do." I survived! It wasn't bad at all. I found the people very accommodating and willing to help.

When we finally arrived in Gadikwa, we headed straight to the Chief's house to let him know we had arrived and that we would set up at the school to talk with young people the following day. The beauty of this job was that I did not have to advertise our services; it was word of mouth, and before you knew it, a crowd had gathered. The local Chief, Kgosi (King) Maezi, welcomed us in his house. He was very kind; he took my hand, looked at it carefully as if he was

Chapter 5: Becoming a Peer Educator

palm reading, and then said to me, "This is a good thing. I have never had a Zambian person in my house. Welcome. You will sleep in my daughter's bedroom." I was moved by his genuine welcome remarks. I did not have to go and set up at a lodge all by myself. That night we had a good traditional Setswana meal: pounded meat with veggies and phaleshe (maize meal mash).

The Queen Mother prepared water for me to bathe with and said I could wash in my bedroom. When I went to the bedroom, I found two buckets. One with warm water and another big bucket like a big dish, which was empty. I was trying to figure out how I was going to wash without spilling water on the floor. After ten minutes, I went back to the kitchen to tell her I had no idea how I was meant to wash. She came back with me and explained that I had to step in the big bucket, pour some water on my body, scrub and then rinse off. After I had done that, I was to get the bucket with dirty water, pour it into the small bucket and throw it outside.

The following day, the Queen Mother was up very early. She had prepared breakfast, cleaned the surroundings and was ready by six o'clock in the morning. We ate with the family and the Chief came and introduced me to the rest of the village. The main topic of concern to the young people in his village was setting up small micro-businesses; this was difficult, as they did not have the start-up capital.

They spoke about how many of them were heading to the University of Botswana, but some of them just wanted to stay in the village, enjoying their way of life. Those who stayed still wanted to make a living. We spoke about setting up mentoring projects for these young people and how we could get the funds they needed from the government. When I left that village, I felt content with myself. I felt I had made a difference!

I Have the Power

I was the bridge between these young people and the Botswana Government. At one point, we even had the Minister for Local Government come and listen to our presentation. Being a voice for others does not cost you anything. I found that I enjoyed these travels and listening to these young people, but the most satisfying thing about all this was that the Botswana Government was able to make a follow-up and actually support these social ventures.

Chapter 5: Becoming a Peer Educator

You Have The Power

1. When you were a young child, what did you want to do with your life?

   _____

   _____

   _____

   _____

   _____

2. What has been your biggest challenge in life? How have you overcome it?

   _____

   _____

   _____

   _____

   _____

3. Can you list three of your values? How you can use them to help others?

   _____

   _____

   _____

   _____

Chapter 6:

Moving Down Under

> *"The world is a book and those who do not travel read only one page."*
>
> **Augustine of Hippo**

I have always loved travelling and going overseas was a dream come true! Destination: Tilburg, the Netherlands. When I left Botswana, it was about 40 degrees Celsius and arriving in Amsterdam, it was minus three degrees. I was chilled to the bone, but I told myself it was another adventure. Despite the cold, we arrived in Tilburg to a very warm welcome of family and friends.

Just like any new environment, the first thing one has to learn in order to fit in is the language. I found the Dutch people to be very friendly at face value, but then they go do their own thing. The first few months were very hard for me to adjust to my new environment as I did not speak the language very well; in my many attempts to

I Have the Power

learn, I failed miserably. So, I decided to put my energy into my books. I travelled a bit to neighbouring countries, sampled food and drinks and admired their arts and culture, but I still felt alone in a crowded place. It was time to move. I missed the sunshine, the food, the people and speaking English.

When I was 22 years old, I applied for work in Australia with my husband Erik, who is a medical doctor. We were asked where we wanted to go and live in Australia. Our response was anywhere were it is warm, and Western Australia it was. Destination: Kununurra. Coming to Australia was both exiting and nerve-wracking. I was told that the top ten most poisonous snakes all live in Australia and a lot of those creatures that could kill you within three minutes were living in the outback where we were going! As an African-born girl, I could go and camp in the African bush and was not afraid as I knew a lion would not sneak up on me, nor would I step on a snake. I wasn't so sure here. Who would tell what could be hiding in my tent if I went camping in the outback!

Kununurra was love at first sight for me; it could have been the red soil that reminded me of home or the boab and mango trees. I remember going to Blackrock Falls, just past Valentine Springs, for a swim. The water was warm, the sunset was magical, and I told myself I could live here forever and still be happy. I felt the connection to the land before I even got to know the people.

After 12 months in the town, I started feeling insignificant; I'm a person who is always on the go and staying at home, cleaning, cooking and part-time studying wasn't working for me. I fell into a mild depression and started to resent myself, thinking I should be doing more. One day, after taking a shower, I looked in the mirror and could not recognize the person that was staring at me.

Chapter 6: Moving Down Under

I was the girl child; I was making a difference in people's lives. I had a purpose in life and now here I was, not contributing to my community. Looking back, I think the homesickness played a part, too. I missed my friends, even though I had friends in Kununurra. I missed the jeans at Mr.Price's clothes store and the food. I got out of the shower and there I was on the floor, curled in a foetal position, crying my lungs out. I felt like I did not belong here, that I had lost my vision and that I was living someone else's dream, not mine.

After thirty minutes, I thought I could drive to the lake and plunge into it to make it look like an accident. Just the thought of that scared me to death! I immediately called 'Beyond Blue', a counselling help line. The lady I spoke to was very kind and very calm. She counselled me and discussed what I was going through, then asked me to get dressed and to talk with someone about my feelings. I never had the chance to thank her, but she was very nice. I spoke with Erik and he arranged for me to get some counselling. Sometimes you may feel like you are all alone in this world, like no one cares, but if you share your concerns you will be surprised to find that people do care about you and your wellbeing.

That was the beginning of my journey as a social change-maker in Australia. I called Save the Children Australia to ask if they wanted people to help out once a week, as I felt I had too much time on my hands. I also applied to work at the local aboriginal radio station as a broadcaster for a few hours each week. Save the Children was a brilliant platform to get to know what the community was doing. It is one of the best organizations I have worked with and they do so much good work. I found that the work they did in the Kimberley, especially with the indigenous communities, was remarkable.

I was later employed as a sexual health research officer, and this gave me a chance to go around the community to consult with elders, youth and the community at large. I found that the Aboriginal culture had so many similarities with African traditions. For example, the way we relate to each other: my father's brothers are my dads and my mother's sisters are my mums; so in theory, you can never be an orphan in both cultures, because when your biological mother passes away, you still have your second and third mother. My first cousins are my brothers and sisters. I did not have to look very far to see that my community needed more hands to help. On any given night, you would find that the streets would be full of kids. With a population of about 7,000 people, about 90 kids from as young as four years of age would be roaming the streets.

When I went to do more research as to why we had kids on the streets at such a tender age in a developed nation, my findings were quite astonishing. The problems were not like the kind of issues you can just throw money at and expect to go away; my observations were that these were deep-rooted problems that had passed from one generation to the next. These kids could not go home because home was not safe for them to go to. The people at most of these homes would be drunk and some of these kids had seen things kids should never see. It was not that these adults had necessarily wanted to drink their lives away, but they were trying to deal with generations of trauma.

I spoke with several indigenous elders, some of whom were doing very well in the community. One day I had the pleasure of sitting down with a respectable Indigenous elder from Cockatoo Springs, a community with about 40 people. He was born in 1949 and lived outside Ivanhoe Crossing. He was brought up on a station on the Durack, which is now Lake Argyle.

This elder used to be a medical student and was involved in the start of the East Kimberley Aboriginal Medical Service, which was later changed to the Ord Valley Aboriginal Health Service. Their

Chapter 6: Moving Down Under

aim at that stage was to treat patients with minor illnesses and trauma, due to the shortage of staff and doctors at the Kununurra District Hospital. This meant that patients, including the aboriginal population, would have to wait for a long time to be seen by a doctor. The Kimberley always has a shortage of doctors and this has a massive impact on the community. The waiting period to see a doctor can sometimes be three to four weeks, unless you go to the emergency department, in which most patients need to see a doctor immediately.

This indigenous elder had 23 grandchildren and he was part of the 'Stolen Generation'. He explained that this was when they separated the mixed children from their parents, but the children still wanted to be part of the aboriginal community and live with their families. "Men used to care for children. Children need to learn skills from parents. The Authorities took away the responsibility from parents, like smacking kids when they do something wrong to correct them."

He mentioned that it is important to have a strong traditional setting and work with elders and communities for programs to work. "First, we need to understand how to communicate in traditional ways and styles, performing traditional ceremonies," he said. "Talk to young people in different ways." He mentioned that there is a need for proper communication between aboriginal and non-aboriginal people. There is a lack of support from families to help youth make simple choices.

Just like any problem, there is a solution. I sat with him on his veranda as one of his daughters brought us tea, and he asked about my people and how they were doing. We talked about my clan and our way of life, about the connection to the land and how sometimes you can hear the land calling for you, wanting you to go back to the bush and enjoy nature. After we had finished drinking our tea, he asked me to accompany him on a short walk around the corner. There, he pointed out the demarcation of his land. He said to me, "This is my new home. My old home is now under water after we were moved out and they dammed the place. Beyond those hills is the home of my ancestors. I grew up in that place, but now it is just water."

I could feel his pain; I could see that even though he was content with his new home, he missed his old home and traditions. I love spending time with people and I love to learn about cultures and customs. Even though the day was hot and we had flies everywhere, I enjoyed my time. He believed in me, he encouraged me to write about what was happening to his people, so that more awareness was created. He told me about how some people think that his people are a dying breed that is not self-sustaining, but the truth is that these people have gone through so much trauma, the healing process is taking far longer than anticipated.

Looking at a wound on his leg, I began to think about my work. I realized I was part of the problem. We have been trying for so long to fix a wound by putting a plaster on it instead of cleaning the wound first, scraping out the infection, and making sure that we prevent the infection from coming back. It is called the bandage solution. This is what most of us were paid to do. I asked him what the solution would be. He looked at me and smiled, and in his calm voice he said, "Nkandu, here are my possible strategies":

"First, there is need for activities in remote communities, as kids have a lot of potential. We just need to collect them and keep them out of mischief." He and his team had been doing after-school programs, like taking kids fishing and planning survival skills programs during the school holidays. He said it was important to show kids the effects of alcohol, especially those who have lost their culture.

Chapter 6: Moving Down Under

"Kids need to get connected to their land. Kids like fishing and playing basketball and football. Take them to 'bubble bubble' for camping. Take them to the lake as an incentive for good behaviour." That afternoon, I drove back home thinking to myself, *how can I be of significant value to my new community?* I then decided to be an active participant and asked the school if I could help in any way. The Kununurra District High School had a program called 'follow your dream'. I was invited to speak to this group of youngsters in the program a few times to inspire them. These were high achieving indigenous youth.

We took them to El Questro for a girl's leadership camp. Kia Dowell was a young indigenous lady that came with us. She achieved many things and had represented her team in New York for her basketball skills. Kia was a change-maker and she is still doing amazing work. She has gone ahead and co-created a commercial aboriginal business. This business involves cultural training, leadership development and cultural capacity building.

This leadership camp was another great way to learn about what the girls were going through. We had about 40 young girls from the Kimberley. Gandwa, an aboriginal organization teaching young people about sports and healthy eating, organized the leadership camp. My main role was to inspire the kids and share my story as a young change-maker; why I do what I do and my passion in life. Like any sessions of mine, I like to hear about you first, so I gave out Smarties and we played the Smarties game: you can eat all the Smarties you want, but leave only one. Depending on the colour you got, you will share something with the group. It could be your last movie, a place you would like to visit or your favourite colour. This icebreaker is easy, fun and everyone loves it. I talked about my journey as a girl child, and why I joined Save the Children.

I Have the Power

When we shared our stories, one of the indigenous students decided to focus on aboriginal health. She had found some fantastic anecdotal evidence to share on the topic. She wanted to do nursing after finishing school, which was very appropriate for her. She elaborated on the difficulties faced by young people, regarding sensitive health issues. Kids could not go to the local Aboriginal Health Service to talk about sexual health, as members of their family would be working there. Discussing sexual and reproductive topics could have consequences for them within their families and possibly the wider community.

I consider these youth as our champions. They can see the problem and they think about solutions and what they need to do to make things better in their communities.

Another remarkable young lady was looking into government initiatives and education. She talked about the disconnect between the money that was coming in and how it was spent. She believed that irresponsible spending in the community encourages a culture of apathy that children absorb and imitate. I remember she was blaming the government for this, not the parents. Her main idea was that there is lack of ambition—not because the government is too charitable, but because there is no encouragement for growth. Another student was looking at entertainment in Kununurra; she was looking closely at how the lack of entertainment for young adults in Kununurra can lead to antisocial behaviour.

The more I spoke and participated actively in the community, the more I found myself sitting with game changers and having tea with local council members. One of the most profound chats was with another indigenous man. This time I had decided I wanted to learn some more English and had enrolled myself in an education program, Open Colleges Australia, just to improve my writing skills. English is my third language, so any opportunity that comes up for

Chapter 6: Moving Down Under

me to learn some more English, I'll take it. I was invited by ABC Open to contribute to Kimberley ABC Open. The idea was to speak to a stranger and get to know him or her a bit. After the program had finished, I went ahead and continued talking to people. I wanted to talk to this aboriginal man who was very successful at what he did, but it seemed he never had enough time to sit and talk with me. I wanted to find out why he was doing very well while most of his people were living in poverty. Yet here he was, working to improve his people's lives. I wanted to find the missing link; I guess it's like that in most places around the world, Africa included.

I finally managed to get an hour with him. He had lived in Kununurra since 1978. His mother was one of the 'Stolen Generation'. The children were sent first to Moola Bulla Station, and then on to the Orphanage in Broome where, 19 years later, he was born. He believes he will be living in or around Kununurra for the rest of his life. "As to what will be keeping me here, a very strong connection to family, friends and country." He enjoys reading, camping, fishing, all sports and crosswords. I asked him what he would like to see change in Kununurra.

"Less racism and more involvement by local indigenous people in employment, training and business enterprises. State and Federal Service Providers providing a higher standard of service. The community in general having a holistic approach to domestic violence and juvenile delinquency as this has a ripple effect on everybody, not just the immediate families." I still agree with this man as most of my indigenous friends felt discriminated against in their own land. Sometimes it seemed like a case of black and white, but we have to be very careful when dealing with such issues. I found the indigenous people of Kununurra welcoming and I could walk and talk in their communities freely. I was accepted and I did not feel judged. I guess it comes back to how you treat people.

I Have the Power

Since arriving in 1978, he had seen Kununurra expand from a small country town similar to Broome, where he grew up, to an industry-driven centre of the East Kimberley. I asked him what his vision was: he said he would like to see more mining companies in the region in the next 50 years, development of the tourism industry, increased farmlands and small businesses supported to improve living standards all over the East Kimberley.

"Although the opportunities have been and still are there, the disappointing thing is that the local aboriginal people have not been a part of this growth through partnerships or business initiatives." This aboriginal elder is a hard-working man, talking about self-discipline and going after his dream.

> "There is no greater gift you can give or receive than to honor your calling. It's why you were born and how you become most truly alive."
>
> **Oprah Winfrey**

After six years in the community having run workshops in leadership development for youth, I was also running Nkandu's lunchtime show at Waringarri Aboriginal Radio Station. The show was inviting community members and leaders to talk about Kununurra and how we could make lives better. During my five years as a presenter, I interviewed a lot of community members and met national leaders

Chapter 6: Moving Down Under

such as Governor General Quentin Bryce, the then Prime Minister Mr.Kevin Rudd and his Minister for Youth, Peter Garrett. Later on, I also met the then Prime Minister Ms Julia Gillard. We had 'regulars', as I called them, like Sergeant Scott Moyes from the Kununurra Police; this was a good thing, as it was improving the understanding of the community about the police and their work.

We had the CEO of the Shire of Wyndham East Kimberley, Garry Gaffney, update the community on Shire business. We had Dr. Simon Hemsley come in and talk about health. When my manager at the station asked me to produce a radio program on Otitis Media, an ear infection predominantly in children, I found that this was a preventable disease and yet children were going deaf due to the lack of available information. So as I did interviews with health professionals and local women, I found that the solution was not as simple as the funding body thought it was. For example, they talked about having enough space in the house to avoid overcrowding. How is it possible to stay healthy in a two-bedroom house with one bathroom and toilet with more than 20 people? I developed ads that were simple to understand without medical jargon and got a nutritionist to come to the radio station every week to talk about healthy eating, especially for children.

In 2011, I was invited to represent Australia at the Commonwealth Head of Government meeting. I was one of the 20 Australian delegates. Before I left for Perth, our then-Youth Minister, Peter Garrett, had asked me to find out what issues are affecting young people in my community; I already knew what the issues were: domestic violence, sexually-transmitted infections, suicide, preventable diseases and lack of recreational activities for young people.

When I arrived in Freemantle at the Esplanade, more than a 100 youth were in the hotel. It was very scary, but I had stayed at this hotel several times before, so at least I knew I would not get lost. The first person I met was Francis Ventura, a young man from Melbourne doing remarkable work with refugee kids in the area of mentoring. Francis asked me which country I was from and I mentioned Australia. He looked puzzled and repeated the question. I told him I was from Kununurra. "You don't look like somebody from the Outback because you're wearing high heels and a fancy dress." He put his akubra hat on me and told me, "*Now* you look like someone from the Outback." We became friends and after I changed into my jeans and CHOGM T-shirt, he introduced me to other delegates.

We worked hard for four days and nights, formulating recommendations for the Heads of Governments. We had key messages that we sent out. All 120 delegates representing the Commonwealth countries agreed upon these. What we were asking for was that the Heads of Governments should strengthen their commitment to invest in young people through transparent mechanisms, ensuring access to ICT, education and funding for enterprise development. We strongly recommended that youth should be given an opportunity to participate directly in all levels of decision-making and young people should be the primary agents of peace building in the Commonwealth. We also talked about preventative measures of communicable diseases as opposed to reactive measures for health management and emphasized the urgency of dealing with environmental issues like global warming.

The core recommendation from the Commonwealth Youth Forum (CYF) 2011 was the establishment of an independent youth-led governing body to oversee the administration of a youth development fund. This was our opportunity to work in partnership with Commonwealth Heads of Government to act together to address the needs of all the Commonwealth people, especially

Chapter 6: Moving Down Under

the youth. Sebastian Robertson from Batyr in Sydney, Marcellus Cazaubon working for the education and culture department in Saint Lucia and me presented these above recommendations.

Our then-Prime Minister, Kevin Rudd, introduced us. He struggled to pronounce my name (as usual) and gave me seven minutes to present. The first few minutes, I was very nervous and everybody was quiet. I stopped and looked up and said," This is the toughest audience I've ever had. You are so quiet! What we need from you guys is to meet us halfway by giving us responsibilities and holding us accountable" He laughed and apologized on behalf of Australia for calling Heads of Governments 'you guys'. When I stood in front of more than 150 Heads of Governments and Foreign Ministers to speak on behalf of 1.2 billion youth, it was like a dream come true. I was nervous, I must confess. I was the first to speak. I had my team to back me up and go through the key points that we wanted the leaders to know.

During the time at CHOGM, I met many leaders and young people from around the world who were doing amazing work. Most of them were from Third World countries. Some of them had to work in very tough conditions for example in war-torn countries, but they still managed to do a good job. I came back home pumped and ready to make some real changes. I spoke to my local council about the recommendations and from the responses I got from the young people in my community, I set up the Kununurra Youth Development Programme, a program with different projects, open to all youth, regardless of their cultural, educational or social background.

A lot of youth programs already running in Kununurra, were focussing on specific groups. I made a program with projects that would welcome anyone who wanted to become a change-maker. I managed to get support from our local council and that made the difference between success and failure. This program was successful, not because I had integrated indigenous and non-indigenous youth, but because I had the community working with me. I had the help of local service providers. When I wouldn't know something, I would ask. I'm not afraid to ask questions; sometimes I would ask a similar question, just to make sure I got it right.

The first meeting I held in my house with likeminded people, as I needed to create a mastermind team. This team included people from different sectors in the community. I had support from Save the Children Australia, from a media company, from Kununurra District High School, from Kununurra District Hospital and from Kenneth Bin Jacob, a local aboriginal artist, who was willing to come and help me run art sessions for both aboriginal and non-aboriginal youth. Boab Health came in to run some nutritional sessions; Judy Hendrikse travelled from Perth to give dance classes; Tamali Howard gave modelling classes; other members of the community helped with different other things, like provision of a sound system and providing a venue.

I found my local council very helpful; I would drop in at the Shire Youth Centre and talk to Sue Gaffney, who was in charge of youth services, about my plan; she would advise me on the best possible strategies; sometimes all she did was listen, but most of the time she would pick up the phone and have the answer to my problem like getting a venue for our programs. We were fortunate Vicky Biorac, from B Visual Media, was able to mentor our youth, teaching them practical skills in media arts and later producing a documentary, which is still on YouTube.

All of this would not have been possible without the support from the government. I came home wanting to make a change, a real change. I had no money and nowhere from which to start,

Chapter 6: Moving Down Under

so I wrote a letter to the Premier, telling him what I had learned and mentioned the people that had inspired me. Within a week, I received a letter from his office, inviting me to go to Perth and talk with our then-Youth Minister, Robyn MacSweeney, and Director General for Youth, Stewart Reid. The meeting went so well that I got double the funding I had requested. We had mentors, a place to run our programs, funding and community support.

At the end of the programs, we had a youth performance to show the community what we had learned; there was dancing, modelling, a photo exhibition and screening of the documentary. We were happy to have Luke Carol as our master of ceremony. I found that my strongest talent lies in communication. You never lose by giving; you only lose by holding back.

You Have The Power

1. Do you know any indigenous people in your community and have you thought of starting a conversation with them to learn something new about their culture?

   _____

   _____

   _____

   _____

2. If you could get a chance to advocate for a group in your community or country, what kind of issues would you be an advocate for?

   _____

   _____

   _____

   _____

   _____

3. Have you ever thought of writing to your local youth minister about issues that affect young people in your area?

   _____

   _____

   _____

   _____

Chapter 6: Moving Down Under

Chapter 7:

Honouring My Calling

> "You must be willing to face all the challenges that come your way and make a special effort not to be discouraged, determination has its rewards."
>
> **Unknown**

> "What I see, I remember. What I hear, I might forget. What I do, I know. Everything about learning is not known, but the law that learners learn through self-experience is everlasting."

I Have the Power

I can remember my first conference as a teenager—it was about Media Ethics and Law. This conference was being held in Botswana Gaborone at the Oasis Motel, a lovely motel with great food and good customer service. What I thought I knew about Media Ethics was not sufficient for me to practice as a media practitioner. At that stage, I realized that school could only teach you so much. I realized that I had to seek lessons in my everyday encounters, the people I meet, the situations around me and the places that I visit. During that time, I met with many inspiring individuals doing amazing things in Media. MISA (Media Institute of Southern Africa) was advocating for my rights to express myself. I thought I had freedom of speech but freedom comes at a cost, someone has to pay for it. I learned that the MISA had been working hard for people like me to get my voice heard.

My first conference in Australia was with the United Nations Association of Australia (Western Australia). I went as a rural delegate and came back as an Executive Member. The UNAAWA and I have our values aligned. My interest in all this was being empowered to discuss how to achieve the millennium development goals, which were set by the United Nations in 2000. These goals were to:

1. Eradicate Extreme Hunger and Poverty
2. Achieve Universal Primary Education
3. Promote Gender Equality and Empower Women
4. Reduce Child Mortality
5. Improve Maternal Health
6. Combat HIV/AIDS, Malaria and other diseases
7. Ensure Environmental Sustainability
8. Develop a Global Partnership for development.

Chapter 7: Honouring My Calling

I was invited to attend this conference to discuss some strategies on how to deal with these problems. These are issues that are very close to my heart. I would love to see these issues solved. I strongly believe that you do not have to live in a big city to care about such issues. You have the power to change the world to make it a better place for everyone, once you realize that we are all connected and all want the same thing. These issues do not only affect Third World countries. This was a wakeup call for me. I realized that I could do so much more than just write about these issues. I also learned about taking care of my environment and my mental health.

One of the most inspiring young individuals I met was Benson Saulo, who was attending as a guest speaker at the conference and is now the head of the Indigenous Leadership Academy. He is the first Indigenous Australian Youth Representative to the United Nations. He started out in Tamworth, NSW. He made it clear to everyone what his role was: "I'm the not the face of reconciliation" he said, "but one of the 1.8 billion young people throughout the world who understand that our future isn't defined by our borders and boundaries, race or religion, but rather the fundamental belief that I'm my brothers' keeper and I am my sisters' keeper."

> *"What you leave behind is not what is engraved in stone monuments, but what is woven into the lives of others."*
>
> **Pericles 495 BC- 429 BC**

I Have the Power

> *"Many people are talented, but only few distinguish themselves. The ability to rise above lies more in effort than talent."*
>
> **Unknown**

These quotes stand true today as they did back then. Each and every person I meet is very important. Relationships are very important to me and people teach us so much. By interacting with other people, we learn a lot about ourselves too. The best thing we can do for others and ourselves is to be completely content with who we are. The way you treat yourself will determine how others treat you.

Another inspiring individual I had the pleasure of meeting was Rhondah Whitaker. Rhondah is very humble, very gorgeous and has a lovely beaming smile. She spoke about the concept of logic and magic. Logic being the idea of sticking to what you are good at and magic about training your mind to do whatever you want it to do. Magic is being you; logic is research and applied learning. Through these conversations I have learned to trust my intuition and to understand the bigger picture. My life is not just limited to my neighbourhood and I have the ability to dream big and make a huge impact! But it starts with me followed by my community. We grow into our roles: no one ever wakes up in the morning and becomes Barack Obama or Hussein Bolt. We all have to cultivate our talents and do our best in whatever we do. We have to strive for excellence.

One of the most important lessons I learned was about personal branding. This is not only about people aspiring to get into

Chapter 7: Honouring My Calling

businesses or doing some cool job. This applies to each and every one of us. The way you look from the outside says a lot about your character. For me, the way I look always affects the way I feel. I have a particular style that I stick to. On Sundays, I'm happy to be in pyjamas all day if I wish to, but you will never see me in front of a crowd not dressed appropriately.

> *"Dress is a very foolish thing, and yet, it is a very foolish thing for a man not to be well dressed."*
>
> **Lord Chesterfield**

What do you want to be known for? Colour your life, my mother would often say to me; wear your colour of passion. Mine will change depending on the season and what I'm doing, but the colours that I love the most are red, orange and yellow but I also like to wear my little black dresses. Find out what works for you—what is the message you are giving to people about who you are and what you do? What does your Facebook picture say about your character? My father always said to me, what you do today will always affect your tomorrow. You might say, "Well I don't care, YOLO," but the truth is, you are growing up and you will need a job or traineeship at some point. In this digital world, the first thing people do is check your online profile.

In 2013, I won the Creative Innovation Scholarship. This was one of the most exciting things that ever happened to me. The two-day conference was held at Sofitel Hotel in Melbourne. I love Melbourne;

I Have the Power

I love the food, the culture and the people. I could walk down the main streets, make a left turn and I'm in a fancy or strange-looking café with delicious food and beautiful décor.

Ci2013 was themed 'Race to the Future' and Scott Anthony, a strategic transformation and innovation expert, based in Singapore, ran one of the sessions I attended. At that stage, I was trying desperately to revive my Youth Empowerment Program Australia and turning it into a structure that was self-reliant and sustainable. He mentioned that most start-ups fail because of premature scale by growing too fast and doing too many things at once. I immediately thought to myself, *yes that's me*. My project had worked successfully in WA, but I was struggling to keep it up in Victoria. I was mentoring kids in Adelaide and being an ambassador for two large organisations all at once. I had put my hand up for almost everything that came my way. I could feel that I was losing focus, but I continued to put my fingers in so many pies.

Key thing to watch out for when starting a new venture is that it's very easy to get confused! It's also very easy to run out of fuel; sometimes we have the passion but not the competence. So how do you use your skills to make this place a better world for everyone to live in? We have 900,000 'not for profit' organizations in Australia, so setting up another 'not for profit' is something I would not encourage right now. NFPs have a lot that need to go into it but they are highly rewarding. How about setting up a social venture where you are making profit for a purpose? That would be a business idea, making you better off, but you will still need to work extra hard. The revolution never starts at the top. Don't ever get sucked up by the crowd. One of the best ways to get lost is to follow what everyone is doing, including fashion and popular trends. Be a trailblazer and find your standpoint. What makes you tick? Embrace your uniqueness and be authentic.

Chapter 7: Honouring My Calling

You Have The Power

1. How do you take the first step to honour your calling?

_____

_____

_____

_____

_____

2. Who are the people in your life who can help

_____

_____

_____

_____

3. What are some of the steps you can take to keep you motivated?

_____

_____

_____

_____

_____

_____

Chapter 8:

Becoming an Official Young Social Pioneer

> *"I seek straight, not to be greater than other, but to fight my greatest enemy, the doubts within myself."*
>
> **P.C. Cast**

So often during my life, I have doubted my capabilities. I have had major insecurities about what I should do, what I could do, and what I actually was doing. When Gary Gaffney, CEO of Shire of Wyndham East Kimberley, sent me the email to apply as a Young Social Pioneer, I immediately jumped on the Foundation for Young Australians' website to look at the past year and what they do on their website. I found that this project would not only be a stepping-stone to my career, but I would also make life-long connections and get the courage to do better than my best. Young Social Pioneers is a leadership program by the Foundation for Young Australians, which is dedicated to unleashing and celebrating the brilliance of young Australian social change-makers. The program runs for 12 months and invests in and supports inspired change-makers aged 18 to 29. YSP provides mentoring, rigorous peer learning, skills development, leadership inquiry and international connections so that we can make a greater impact.

Looking at the FYA website and their alumni, I strongly felt underqualified; so many mixed emotions were going through my head. The application process was not that difficult, but I did not finish it until the last minute. This was not because I couldn't write it up in one day, but because I felt I wouldn't make it by comparing myself to the previous game changers around the country. I had put a label on myself as someone who could not be on the same level as the alumni.

The truth is, when you tell yourself that you are worthless often enough, you begin to believe it. What we feed our minds is very important. A few days before the closing date, I got a call from FYA to ask me to finish my application, as they wanted to hear more of what I was doing. At that point, I did not think much about it but I finished the application anyway and submitted it. I was told they had more than 150 applications. When I got a 'congratulations' email, informing me I was in the top 100, I thought that was it. Who gets excited to be in the top 100? After a few days, it came to 50, then 30. This was the time I knew this was serious business.

When I got the telephone interview, I was very nervous. Twenty-eight candidates were all called for a face-to-face interview and 18 were selected, including me. Most candidates were flown into Melbourne but for me, coming from Kununurra WA that would be at least a 4-day return trip via Darwin; maybe Sydney or Alice Springs. Instead of having the interview in Melbourne, it was organized in Perth. I had no idea what to expect when I arrived in Perth other than

Chapter 8: Becoming an Official Young Social Pioneer

sitting with previous pioneers and someone from FYA. I absolutely lack a sense of direction, so I gave myself some extra time to the venue from my hotel, but I still managed to arrive late, which was a blessing in disguise.

The hotel receptionist gave me directions, completely opposite to where I had to be; the venue of the interview was showing only a five-minute walk, but after 15 minutes of walking, I decided to ask for help. It was cold and it had just stopped raining. I was wearing a pink dress with a white belt and was barefoot, holding my pink and white high heels in my hands. A gentleman made a comment that a girl dressed that beautifully should not be walking barefoot in the city! I wanted to make an impression during the interview and I of course needed to be on time! That just meant I had to take my shoes off as no one walks that fast in heels on a wet surface.

So, I finally arrived at my destination and had to wait! This was a great relief. I had no idea I was going to meet one of the most significant Australian women at the time, Jan Owen. I had heard of Jan Owen, but had never met her. When we had the interview, I spoke about what it was like to be in the Kimberley and the challenges and triumphs my community was experiencing. The following weeks were quite stressful. After that meeting, I knew this program would be a great stepping-stone for my future as a social change-maker. I got one more telephone interview, followed by an email to congratulate me on becoming a Young Social Pioneer.

The first person I thanked was Mr. Gary Gaffney, as he was the one who had sent me the email in the first place. When I had so many doubts about myself, he made me believe in myself again. FYA sent out a media release indicating the chosen YSPs and that was when things got really serious. We had training in media skills, capital raising, leadership skills, self-care, turbo-charging your venture and additional firsthand learning from the world's best in different sectors of social change and enterprise.

Sometimes all it takes is someone to believe in you. The fact that other people believed in me is what got me going. The journey of being a Young Social Pioneer was wonderful, and I have been taught skills and knowledge that would have taken me years to master on my own. The connections are some of the most valuable things I got.

Being one of the 18 young change-makers was humbling. Who would have thought that a girl born in a small country town in Zambia would be a change-maker in Australia? I did dream big; I am a dreamer and I love living, but never had I imagined my life would have turned out this way. All the Young Social Pioneers have done wonderful jobs, past and present; the standards keep rising every year and more and more young social change-makers are emerging with brilliant innovations to create positive change. You are never too young or too old to make a difference. You can do it, as you have so much power within you. I guess life is a journey of continuous discovery of oneself.

The Commonwealth Youth Forum taught me so much as a person; I always have been confident that I have what it takes to succeed, but we all have that little voice that says, "You are not experienced. You shouldn't be here. You are an imposter." Guess what: tell those little voices to shut up and sit down. Your mind can never have two emotions going at the same time. It's either you are in a good mood or a bad mood, and that is what determines our success.

Learning from more than 120 change-makers from across the Commonwealth and shaping the future of the Commonwealth is quite an experience and if I could do that, you can do that too, and much greater things. You can inspire others to reach their greatness.

Chapter 8: Becoming an Official Young Social Pioneer

Having an opportunity to have an education is a privilege. I have had conversations with my friends who say it's a right, but the fact is, more than half of the population on earth has no access to clean water, let alone education facilities.

I often compare developed nations with developing nations and ask myself, "What would happen if we concentrated on trade instead of aid?" Most of the young people that I have met want to trade. They want to learn skills and contribute to the development of their country instead of simply be given handouts! What would happen if most schools in Africa taught science from an early age? I strongly believe that denying young people the ability to properly develop their knowledge in science is setting them up for failure.

I Have the Power

Chapter 8: Becoming an Official Young Social Pioneer

You Have The Power

1. What are some of the programmes you can apply for in your state that would add to your personal and professional development?

   _____

   _____

   _____

   _____

2. Local councils are usually well equipment with resources around youth development and community development in general. What steps can you take to make a relationship with your local council?

   _____

   _____

   _____

   _____

3. The Foundation for Young Australians have great initiatives around the country , I encourage you to have a look at their website www.fya.org.au. Which initiative would you like to take part in?

   _____

   _____

   _____

Chapter 9:
A Helicopter View

> "Don't go around saying the world owes you a living. The world owes you nothing. It was here first."
>
> **Mark Twain**

> "Don't judge me, unless you can walk a mile in my shoes."
>
> **Unknown**

I Have the Power

As an African child, I was exposed to death at an early age; serious problems like poverty and starvation were all around us. HIV/AIDS and other diseases have been affecting our continent for quite some time now. Despite all these troubles, I had a perfectly normal childhood. It's not that it was normalized to live amidst all these tragedies but I guess we developed a coping mechanism to deal with such issues and move on to the next thing. Life was simple and straightforward. The concept of living your life as if it each day was your last is true for many people around the world. Some of my friends came to school on an empty stomach. It's not because their parents were lazy, but because the system was set up in a way that makes the rich get richer and the poor poorer.

As I would walk to school, I came across houses without running water, others with broken sewer systems and some with many holes and crumbled walls. Despite this, the people found a way of living and still managed to smile and greet each other with respect despite the very high death rates, especially amongst the very young. I guess that's one of the best things of living in Africa: people are genuinely happy and they are concerned about your welfare, which I experienced during my travels.

I believe poverty can bring out the worst in people. Lack of basic amenities and learning opportunities are forces working against us, especially when it comes to education. Girls are less likely to get an education in Africa. Most parents would rather send a boy to school than a girl. There are some terrorist groups that are working very hard to stop girls from going to school. They threaten these girls, burn schools and sometimes even kidnap them so they do not have access to a modern education.

Education is such a privilege and the best way you can give back or help other people is by educating yourself first in whatever way you can. We all know that if a girl gets a basic education,

Chapter 9: A Helicopter View

she makes better choices about her life; she delivers fewer babies and her chances of survival increase. She gets to contribute to her community and development of her country. In Botswana, we have a saying: "Empower a woman, shield a nation". Millions of girls around the world put their lives at risk just to go to school. I find this overwhelming. I consider myself very fortunate that I can read and write in a foreign language and I have the freedom to do what I want and go wherever I want to go. If you are holding this book, you are one of the fortunate people around the world.

As a child growing up in Africa, I thought we had more than enough. My grandparents were givers, my parents were givers and I thought we were rich. We had a nice house, lived in a nice neighbourhood and my father had a motorbike and a company car. We had a maid, a gardener and a security guard. Most of my friends could not afford all this. My father would give me money to buy shoes just because he could. One day, this got him into trouble, as my mother did not like the idea of buying stuff just for the sake of buying. My mother would only buy necessary things.

I remember a day in Solwezi: we lived in a house behind a bank, right in town and 200 meters from my father's work place. I went into town and saw some nice suede shoes. I went straight to dad's office to ask for money. He was in a board meeting but I still went ahead and asked the secretary to get him out. I could see he was very busy and irritated by my unexpected visit. His first reaction was, "This better be quick, I need to go." My response was, "I need your wallet; I need to buy shoes for me and my sister." He handed over his wallet and asked me not to lose it. "I'll bring it back." I said. "No, I'll be home in three hours; you better be home by then!"

I walked out, bought the shoes and went straight home. When my mother asked me to send the shoes back, as my sister and I did not need any more shoes, I told her Dad had given me his wallet,

101

I Have the Power

which was an endorsement to be allowed to buy anything. When Dad got home that afternoon, Mum was not in her best mood. She explained on how we wasted the money and could have used it for something better, like help pay for someone's school fees.

Education is very important and in Zambia, if your school fees are not paid, you cannot attend school. So my mum imprinted her feeling for community responsibility in me.

This was also the reason I joined the United Nations Association of Western Australia, as I strongly support the Millennium Development Goals, one of them being to achieve universal primary education for every child. The shoes became a big issue and to end the argument, my father said to mum as we were having dinner, "If I don't spoil my children, no one will." Not long after that, the World Bank pulled out of Zambia, for reasons unknown. I knew my father was sponsored by the World Bank to do the work he did, so his company started retrenching workers. It became kind of survival of the fittest.

We moved back to Ndola and I could see the difference in our way of life. My mother became the main income earner; we lost our maid, our security guard and our gardener. We reduced the number of meals sometimes to only porridge for breakfast—plain cornmeal porridge with sugar. We still would get fruits or veggies from our garden and that would be for our recess at school. At times I would have to wear the same uniform all week because we did not have laundry powder. But I knew my parents were working extra hard to put food on the table. My mother would sacrifice her transport money to walk an hour to work and back so that she could spend it to buy food instead. Sometimes she would eat less and give her food to us kids. I saw my father go without food or pass the plate to us so we could eat. Hot showers became a luxury, along with normal bread and butter. I guess sometimes you have to pass

Chapter 9: A Helicopter View

through hardship to appreciate the simple things in life. Despite all the poverty that was in the house and a sense of hopelessness, my parents would still dance. I remember my family would play some music and teach my sister how to dance in the sitting room. My parents tried to make life as comfortable as they could for us.

My father's company went broke quickly, and it was then was time to make a move. A year later, we moved to Botswana, where both my parents had fairly good jobs and our lifestyle went back to what we were previously used to, but this time we had gone through 18 months of living it tough and I found out the hard way not to waste any food or resources.

In May 2013, my friend Daniel Cavanagh invited me to 'Live Below the Line', an initiative of the Oak Tree Foundation in a bid to raise money to end poverty in Third World countries. You use $10 to buy food, which has to last for 5 days, so $2 per day. I was very excited and jumped on board. The idea of 'Live Below the Line' for me was not just to raise money, but also to walk in the shoes of the poor. Thousands of Australians have done this challenge, but for me it was personal. I found myself connecting back with Zambia. The hunger pains were worse than I thought.

When Daniel asked me if I could, my immediate response was of course 'yes'. He then said to me, "Nkandu, I have done this before, it will be very hard and you need to be physically and mentally prepared for this." Armed with my $10, I went to buy food that would last me 5 days. It is not much that you can buy with $10, but I managed to invest in a pack of spinach, a pack of pancake mix, 500g of rice, a tin of beans, an apple, and a few bananas. Day one was very exciting; I was actively supporting one of Australia's best charities! By day two, this is what I wrote on my blog:

Day Two: Live Below the Line

I would like to sincerely thank my sponsors and supporters helping me on this great cause. I would also like to thank Daniel Cavanagh for introducing me to the works of the Oak Tree Foundation and LBL.

The last 24 hours have been a challenge. When Daniel introduced me to LBL, I said to myself, "I'm African, what can be hard about living on two dollars a day! Besides, this can't be worse than labor and I'm from the Australian outback, we are tough!" What I did not realize is how hard it would be and that I would have no choice but wait for my next meal. One important fact! I have watched my portions of food.

My friend Elizabeth invited me for breakfast in town with pancakes and chai lattes and mochas. I sat at the table watching everyone eat, surrounded by food and not being able to touch it. The poorest people can't even afford pancakes and eating out is not an option. Cooking for the family has been tough too! I'm trying to make simple meals. I love cooking and I enjoy food. It's so limited with what one can do on $2 a day. Not much, really. I go to bed and thank God I have a bed, a warm shower and a home. I thank him for the gift of life and all the little things in life that seem insignificant. It's amazing how one's spirit can lift up when you count your blessings.

Chapter 9: A Helicopter View

> *Even though I have lived in Africa for 19 years, it's only now that I truly understand what it means to go without food. It makes me appreciate life even more. I know I can go back to the fridge after three days, but what about those in the poorest corners of the world? The question I'm asking myself is, "Where to from here?" PS: For those trying to lose weight, try living on $2 a day. The downside is you will not have a lot of energy.*
>
> *Live, Love and Inspire!*
>
> *Happy Living,*
>
> *Nkandu Beltz*
>
> *PS: Elizabeth did not eat anything for moral support. Love you, Liz.*

Being African and having experienced hardship does not make you immune to hunger or more hardship. It's about the mindset to change. This experience did not just bring out the hunger, but I felt this immense compassion and I wanted to do more. I knew I could go back to my fridge anytime and eat what I wanted; I knew I could always ring up a food delivery service to drop me a pizza or whatever I wanted. But the realization that millions of people live in impoverished conditions and most of them of them in Africa was heartbreaking. After day five, I began a gratitude journal. I was and still am grateful for the gift of clean water, for my clean bed and the ability to wake up in the morning with the sun shining.

I Have the Power

I look at rain as a blessing. At times life seems harsh, unfair and we look at other people and think they are living large and having the best of everything. But the truth is, we all have our insecurities; we are all fighting our own battles. We are not in a competition as to who is winning at this game called 'life'; that's not what we are here for. I'm not sure what your purpose is, but take the time to find it. You might say, who am I to make a difference? You will come up with a million excuses as to why you shouldn't do what you want to do, but you can match that list with why you should do what you want to do. Look at Nick Vujicic. When I first saw his YouTube clip, I said to myself, "Surely, what has he got to be happy about?" But the more I read his books, the more I found that happiness is a choice; we do not choose the circumstances we are born in, but we choose how we respond to the cards life throws at us. Just like all these hundreds of millions of human beings around the word who did not choose to be born in Third World countries under such conditions, but often they still smile. They go and fetch water and walk for miles, but still smile and appreciate the simple things in life.

I knew I could not help all those people, but as a society we can work together and help the less fortunate. I believe in you, I know you have the power to help other people! You have the power to do great things with your life! I know you have the power to use your talents and skills to make someone's life better. Just by doing small things, little steps will make big changes. You are blessed beyond measure; you have so much to give in life. Take the time to write down at least 10 things you are grateful for, you will be surprised what this little exercise can do. Gratitude is such a wonderful gift and every morning I wake up and I go through my gratitude list. I can see the difference: when I just stumble out of bed into the shower and off to do my daily tasks, I feel unbalanced, but when I center myself and focus my thoughts to work with me, I feel much better. When someone says: "Good morning Nkandu, how are you

Chapter 9: A Helicopter View

today?" My response is always, "I am great thank you, and how are you?" I do this with a smile.

Smiling is a universal language that says, "I'm so happy to see you." I smile at everyone. Sometimes it becomes a bit awkward, smiling to strangers, but it makes me happy. I smile at security guards when I'm at the airport, I smile at taxi drivers when I stop a cab and I smile at doctors when I'm admitted in hospital, even though I'm in pain. I have pictures of me smiling in the theatre, and also just before and after I've undergone an operation with general anesthetic. For me, a smile says, "I'm here, I care and I'm happy to see you." 'Live Below the Line' not only changed my perspective on life and practicing gratitude, it helped me to not judge other people. We often ask why it is that poor people are even poor, and we judge them for it.

When I was in grade 11, my friends and I won a school debate as to why people are poor. We argued that they are poor because it's their own fault; we did so to win the debate. Even from a very young age, I realized that this world needed more compassionate people to reach out and help others. Not by giving handouts, but by giving skills and doing trade with poor people and countries, not giving aid!

In other words, you have the power to change things from the way they are. Let your greatness evolve and be expressed.

"Overcoming poverty is not a task of charity, it is an act of justice. Like Slavery and Apartheid, poverty is not natural. It is man-made and it can be overcome and eradicated by the actions of human beings. Sometimes it falls on a generation to be great. YOU can be that great generation. Let your greatness blossom."

Nelson Mandela

Chapter 9: A Helicopter View

You Have The Power

1. Make a list of five blessings that you have in your life right now.

   _____

   _____

   _____

   _____

   _____

2. Who could you thank for their contribution to your life? Have you thanked them?

   _____

   _____

   _____

   _____

   _____

3. If you could give up one thing to help others, what would it be?

   _____

   _____

   _____

   _____

   _____

Chapter 10:

Dreams Continue to Come True

> *"The whole purpose of religion is to facilitate love and compassion, patience, tolerance, humility, and forgiveness."*
>
> **Dalai Lama**

In my life, I have been very fortunate to meet with famous leaders as well as everyday heroes. When I was young and would sit down watching news with my father, I had heard of this great religious leader who had fled his Chinese-ruled homeland for India in 1959 and later won a Nobel Peace prize. I remember saying to myself, "One day, I will shake his hand." In June 2013, I was invited by Foundation for Young Australians to attend the Young Minds Conference. This invitation came with a question: "Tick if you would like to sit with the Dalai Lama on stage." For a moment, I thought this was a joke. If all the application letters had a choice of sitting with the Dalai Lama, surely the stage would be full. Every

I Have the Power

day is a special day for me, but this particular day was extra special because I knew I would be meeting the Dalai Lama! The invitation was to sit with him. We had about 50 other people sitting around with him. I knew I would be shaking hands with him, so I practiced my smile, my handshake, looked in my hotel mirror and smiled back at my reflection. I was at peace with myself. I was content with life.

When I walked to the Sydney Town Hall, my name was not on the list. I took out my registration papers and showed them to the usher, telling him I was one of the people meeting with His Holiness. I needed to be in a special room for briefing. They went through their list and finally found my name.

I knew most of the people in the room. I took my welcome pack and went straight to my seat and after a few minutes, we were at the briefing room with lots of people. We were told only to speak or shake hands upon his invitation. We were then led to the stage were more than a thousand people were sitting behind us. I took my seat right in the middle of the stage. We had an age range from 5 to 30 years.

The proceedings went very well. His Holiness sat in the middle of the stage, having his back slightly turned at me. But when he walked in, he looked me in the eye and I looked back straight at him with a smile and he smiled back. I felt like I knew him; something about his smile that made me feel happy.

I was invited to come and sit next to him and ask him a question. As I walked toward the stage, I could feel that all eyes were on me. Trust me, I don't have many insecurities about myself, but I was very nervous. Every step towards him became heavier until he stretched out his hand. That was a welcome that made me feel so comfortable. We shook hands and he gestured for me to sit down. He even came closer as I spoke with a soft voice. He looked me

Chapter 10: Dreams Continue to Come True

in the eye for the second time and I stayed fixed on his eyes. I felt completely calm and suddenly everything was quiet. It was like time stood still and we were the only people in the entire universe. At this time, he was still holding my hand. The positive energy just rushed right through me. Nothing could disturb my inner peace and when he asked me what my name was, my response was calm, "My name is Nkandu Beltz. I'm coming from Country Victoria." I then went on to ask my question, "So Your Holiness, what is your personal opinion on people who use religion as a way of oppressing and abusing women?"

I was expecting an answer from a Buddhist background, but he looked at me and said, "I think they are backwards. No religion is meant to oppress or abuse women and children." He went on to explain that this should not be happening at all. Everyone is born free and everyone should live freely. He has a holistic approach to life. He shared with the audience about how each and every individual should be given an equal chance to blossom and to live up to one's potential.

He talked about the basic needs for a human being to be happy and the rest comes second. I have been a big follower of the Dalai Lama for a very long time. I have followed his teachings and I love the way he talks about compassion and gratitude. It is from his teachings that I learned to take things as they are. Life is just life and we have to do what we can with it. Be humble and treat other people with respect. But my dream of meeting him had become reality!

That afternoon, after the conference had finished, my friends and I went to Swissotel on Market Street. I had the best hot chocolate in my life. Everything was great and life was magnified 100 times better. I had people stopping me wanting to shake my hands, just because I had been that close to His Holiness. I felt he is a very nice man and he knew I was afraid. He had to calm me down and I know he is very kind to everyone. It is such a shame that the politics in his country are making it very difficult for him to travel and do what he can do. He is seen as a political threat. But regardless of what China says or does, he will still be one of the most influence leaders of our time.

The whole experience with His Holiness was a beautiful reminder of how one can make a huge impact by using non-violence methods to change the world. I had my five minutes of fame, sitting next to him and holding his hand but the truth is, for me, the most important thing was how he made me feel. How we treat other people is very important, first impressions do matter. You do not need a high position to treat people with respect. It does not matter where they come from, what they have done, or where they are going. Imagine if we could all just treat each other with a little extra kindness and understanding. It's better to be slow in judging and forgive easily. Life is so much easier when you finally understand who you are and what makes you tick. The best simple exercise that I do is my journal of self-discovery.

I find writing down everything that I have done, everything I want to do and everything I am doing gives me a much better perspective on who I am. You can never treat others with respect and love if you do the opposite to yourself. Once you embrace who you truly are and honor your calling in life, you will be at peace with yourself. His Holiness is a perfect example. He did not choose to be the Dalai Lama and he did not fight his calling. He simply embraced it and touched and motivated so many people around the world, advocating for freedom and peace.

It's great to be paid doing what you do, implementing what you're passionate about and living your dreams, but even if you're not, life can be very rewarding, so enjoy it. When I was working as a radio broadcaster in Kununurra, I could not believe I was getting paid to

Chapter 10: Dreams Continue to Come True

have so much fun. I loved my work so much, every working day of my life was just magical. It didn't seem like work at all. But that was because I knew I was making a difference in my community.

From a very young age, heroes and she-roes have inspired me! In our African customs, our family upholds certain values. One of the values is 'Botho', a Setswana term. Botho is a value that each and every African child should possess and express; our elders say that Botho incorporates the qualities of a human being, including kindness, good manners, compassion, humility, respect for others and living up to one's responsibilities.

Recently, I have been following what has been happening in some African countries with respect to gay rights and homosexuality. As a girl child advocate and a child brought up in a Christian family with values of compassion and tolerance, it was quite disheartening to realize the kind of crimes inflicted on fellow human beings with different views and beliefs. I wasn't surprised with His Holiness, the Dalai Lama's view on gay rights, considering his secular and holistic response on domestic violence towards women when I spoke with him. I admire his courage and boldness to condemn homophobia and agreeing that if the sex is consensual, it is ok. Other influential leaders like South Africa's Archbishop Desmond Tutu have expressed similar views.

We have a responsibility to care for and love our fellow human beings. Despite having traditions and religions, people should make up their own minds and do what is right. For so many years in our history books, black people and other minorities were treated so badly. Our ancestors fought for freedom, for our rights to vote and for women to be equal to men. Humanity has come so far and we have advanced in so many ways. I encourage you to have some compassion and love for those people who are different from you.

I Have the Power

Every person we meet will leave an impression with us. Sometimes we are in awe of these souls and sometimes we are glad that they left our side. I was once told that people come into your life for many reasons. Some people are meant to stay, others will just pass by and even though relationships come and go, it's always for the best. It means you can do with or without that person. Some are there to stay in your life to help you move higher in your personal pursuit of your dreams.

While I was in Botswana at Maun Senior Secondary School, I had great teachers. This included the principal of the school, who was a remarkable, wise man. My teacher of literature, Mr. Price, was funny and made everyone feel great about themselves, including me so I loved being in his class. We could study a book and talk about the country and people depicted in the book. I remember us talking about India, the colors of food and the people on the streets after reading Malgudi Days by R.K. Narayan. The words in the book came alive and I fell in love with the words as I could transfer myself into the book.

Another teacher who impacted my life greatly was Mr. Simon Hopkins, who was initially our English teacher, but later also our religious education teacher, after one of the other teachers, Mr. Conteh, died. He was always calm and respected everyone around him. Our peers in other schools were two years ahead in religious education when I took up the subject, which was when another teacher died, my French teacher, Mr. Reid. When this happened, our Principal took it upon himself to teach us French. After a few weeks, we all knew this wasn't going to work, so I dropped out of French class and changed to religious education. It was an educational requirement that students needed to study more than one language, and French was the only option under the circumstances, but we could not continue. I knew I had to study very hard to pass this subject and Mr.. Hopkins used his spare time to explain the

Chapter 10: Dreams Continue to Come True

curriculum to me. He would take time after hours to see students who needed help, and I was one of those students. I still appreciate the huge effort and sacrifice he made to help me pass my religious education!

Teachers play an important role in our lives and I had teachers who believed in me and made extra effort to help me and listen to my ideas. That gave me extra confidence. I was told that I was like a butterfly that cannot be caged and needs to fly high. We learn lessons through self-experience, attending classes, playing on playgrounds, participating in conferences and communicating in everyday life from our interaction with fellow humans. We leave a mark on each other's hearts either through a smile, a warm hug, a gentle touch, kind words, or through just listening to what someone has to say.

As I sat next to His Holiness with him holding my right hand, he made me feel comfortable and at peace, not only with myself, but also with the rest of the world. I hope one day I can do the same for someone else.

You Have The Power

1. If you could meet with a world leader, who would it be? Why?

_____

_____

_____

_____

2. What would you like to ask him/her? What would you love to learn or know?

_____

_____

_____

_____

3. What are some of the global issues that you care about and why?

_____

_____

_____

_____

_____

Chapter 11:

You are Perfect with Your Imperfections

> "Let go of who you think you're supposed to be and embrace who you are."
>
> **Brené Brown**

> "Today, I made a new best friend; she listened to everything I had to say. She did not judge me at all. When I had finished, I moved closer as I wanted to hug her, then I realized my new best friend was a mirror."
>
> **Unknown**

I Have the Power

When I started high school, I felt increasingly insecure about my body. This was because of the comments that peers were making about me. I thought I was too thin, I thought my legs were too long, I thought my face was way too pretty and that I was a disruption to the boys in my class. I started to believe the outside influence that was coming in. I would eat sweet potatoes for breakfast and lots of maize and bread; whatever calories I could find in the house. But my weight would remain the same. After a chat with my father, he reassured me that nothing is wrong with me and that I had to accept who I was and the way I was.

These insecurities are brought upon us from the outside world. This is because we immediately start to compare our lives with others. I used to do that. I would ask myself how come my friends are growing boobs and I'm not? Instead I should have been telling myself that I'm a unique being, that I will blossom at my own time and let nature take its cause. I heard Napoleon Hill say in his audiobook today that criticism is like water on a duck's back, and that he is not affected by it at all. How is it possible that someone can have such a strong mental attitude? You are perfect just the way you are. It has taken me years to be fully content with my body image and my capabilities and limitations, but I also knew that certain things need to be learned. Certain things need skills and just like any skill, you can learn them.

No one is perfect, but we are all born perfect in our own way. Your circumstances do not define you; your character does. The best way to sum all this up is by counting your blessings, learning the skills you need to learn in order to advance yourself and those around you.

When I was in grade 11, I remember sitting outside my classroom at Maun Senior Secondary School playing truth or dare. My friend dared me to enter the upcoming beauty contest. I did it out of fun.

Chapter 11: You are Perfect with Your Imperfections

I was not prepared, but the whole experience was very exciting: the makeup, the dress, the music and the crowd cheering. I didn't make it past the third round, but I wasn't in it to win.

I felt that after that experience, I gained a certain amount of self-confidence. I was introduced to high heels, which I love dearly to this day. There are certain things that a girl needs, and for me, heels are little accessories that I like to wear every now and then. At 16, I began looking at my life differently. I would look in the mirror and smile, and look at my legs and thank God I had legs. I would look at my scars and think of how I got those scars—most of them from falling off trees and cooking in the kitchen. Those were memories. I realized that each and every scar on my body had a story.

The more I appreciated what I had and what I could do, the more I cherished those around me. I began to realize that my happiness was dependant on others. If I could make someone happy, I would be happy. I knew, I had done my best, even if the other person did not appreciate my best, then so be it, you cannot please everyone. I made it my mission to look at my imperfections and love them the way they are. I made a conscious decision to stop pleasing others because of their expectations and started doing things for myself because I wanted to do those things.

> *"Where there is light, you will find a shadow."*
>
> **Michelle Beltz**

I Have the Power

When Michelle said this to me, I thought to myself, "What wise words." We often focus on the light and try to hide from our shadows but if we can embrace our light and darkness and treat these two the same, we will then have a balance in our lives, like Yin and Yang.

One day, while attending a meditation class, an Indian Guru asked me, "Who are you?" I said I was a journalist. She said, "No, that's *what* you are." I said I was a mum, she said "No," again. "That's *what* you are…!" She asked me to go home after the session to have a think about it. I spent hours thinking about her words and then I realized that everything that I thought I was, or what I thought described me, was just part of me. As I lay my head on my pillow, the answer came to me. It was like someone was talking to me, "Nkandu, you are a tiny particle in the Universe. You are just as important as the air that you breathe, the water that you drink and land you walk on." I realized I was part of this Universe and my existence and whole being is integrated in this Universe. I was very content with that because I realize that my past, my mistakes and my accomplishments did not define *who* I was but *what* I was. What matters is the now, not the past! The fact that you and I are one and everyone is connected.

Gratitude is the greatest way of finding happiness.

Chapter 11: You are Perfect with Your Imperfections

> "To the barefoot man, happiness is a pair of shoes. To the man with old shoes, happiness is a new pair of shoes; to the man with new shoes, it's more stylish shoes and of course the fellow with no feet would be happy to be barefoot. Measure your life by what you have, not by what you don't."
>
> **Michael Josephson**

> "The way you look at yourself is the way others will treat you."
>
> **Nkandu Beltz**

> "Confidence is tied up with simplicity. If you express yourself simply, it inspires confidence."
>
> **Stephen Bayley & Roger Mavity**

Confidence or positive self-esteem is not something people are born with. It is a skill and just like swimming, confidence can be learned. This means being able to speak up, present and deal with issues as they come; to be able to make decisions and to take reasonable risks. But you have to make a choice and you have to practice every day. I can say that I have certain areas of my life where I'm pretty confident, but I also get moments when self-doubt creeps in. This is when you need to be prepared and change those negative thoughts into positive ones. In my case, music helps. I love to dance. If I'm feeling anxious or about to step on stage, I will play my favourite song and sing with it. But the night before an event, I picture myself on stage, smiling and everyone smiling with me. I use this technique with everything: if I walk into a boardroom and I'm feeling intimidated, I just say fresh its like saying cheese, leaving a nice gentle smile on your face to myself, which puts a smile on my face and I sing my song silently.

People can feel your fear, but you always have to remember why you are in that position in the first place. In my life, I found that it was easier for me to build self-confidence and understanding of myself by having positive role models. Some of these people were my peers; others were older. I would read books that made me

Chapter 11: You are Perfect with Your Imperfections

laugh, and I would only associate with peers who wanted the best out of life. I've never had time to sit idle and wait for the sun to set. We all have a purpose in life, but before finding this, you need to be able to find people you trust and respect; someone who will help you build up your confidence and will not judge you or abuse you in any way.

I have had strong mentors from a very young age. I have always asked for guidance and still do. In Africa, we have a proverb: "If you see a tortoise sitting in the top of a tree, someone helped it get there." We cannot achieve massive success by playing solo. We need a mastermind team to support us. We need an empowering and caring community. We need people who care, but how do we find them?

They are all around you. They are your teachers, parents, friends, neighbours, colleagues and people at your local sports club. Take the time to go out and meet people in safe environments. I find that most people, when they move to a new country, tend to isolate themselves. They have so many excuses as to why they are not part of the community. Some of the excuses I have been told are: "English is my third language," "They don't understand what I have to say," "I don't know anyone," "I'm the only black girl in the club," "But I have never played footy in my life," and so on.

Well, you are right! It's because you have never tried. You always have an opportunity to learn. Any skill can be learned. Isolation is one of the most damaging traumas to a human being. It does not matter if you newly arrived in a community or you have lived all your life in one location; you need to get up and meet other people. When I was in high school, I came across a book called *Chicken Soup for the Teenage Soul*. I thought the book was in the wrong section of the library, but when I turned it around to read the back,

I Have the Power

I was captivated by the words and immediately began to read the book. When I finished the first book, I continued the series.

What I realised through reading nonfiction books and talking to my friends about teen problems was that I wasn't so unique when it comes to such problems. I realized I didn't own all the problems in the world and a lot of problems just seem yours only, but actually are very common. How do you overcome your first crush? Does this T-shirt look good on me? I'm so ugly with all these zits; who will ever like me? But as we grow older, we begin to focus on more concrete solutions and how we can make better decisions to help other people. My sister sent a text on what her seven cardinal rules of life. I read them and smiled, but then I thought what my *eight* cardinal rules of my life were:

1. *Letting go*. I have learned to let it go. Sometimes things happen to us and we ask ourselves: why me? Why did he say what he said? What did he mean? Why didn't I make a smarter decision? You have to accept what happened and not feel defeated.

2. *People will always say something about me*. I learned this when I was in high school. I would get comments like "Nkandu orate dilo," a Setswana phrase used to describe people who are self-centred and narcissistic. This happened because of my public appearances and advocacy. Some people did not understand why certain things needed to change.

   I remember going to the principal's office in tears because one of the teachers had accused me of having a sugar daddy as I'd had a cell phone in the class and in those days, students couldn't afford mobile phones. The phone belonged to my father. He'd said to me, "Nkandu, people will always talk about you. If you don't give people something to talk about, they will make something up, but it's up to you to let it affect you or not."

Chapter 11: You are Perfect with Your Imperfections

3. *Time heals everything*. I don't think this statement is true, but from my experience, time helps to put things in perspective. All the drama we go through in life never get any easier and having lost many loved ones in my life, the pain is still the same, but as time goes on, I have learned to accept the loss and to keep beautiful memories.

4. *Never compare yourself to others*. This is a hard one. I used to ask myself this question all the time, "How come I'm not succeeding fast enough?" I would look at what my peers are doing and try to beat them at my game until I realized that I'm not in competition with anyone. It's my life.

5. *Stop thinking too much*. This is what slowed down some of the progress I could have made, especially when it comes to business decisions. I thought I was a 'plunger' when it comes to making decisions, but I realize that I sometimes accept negative, 'logical' advice and stop following my intuition like when I did not go into a partnership out of fear of losing my credibility. Sometimes it's just best to sit quietly, listen to your heart and let the answer come to you.

6. *You are 100% responsible for your actions,* and that includes your happiness. This applies to relationships, too. I often hear people say, "But he made me do it" or "I was so upset, that's why I said what I said." The truth is you are 100% responsible for *your* actions. Every relationship is a 50/50 but 100% responsibility on each part.

7. *Smiling*. This is my favourite. Sometimes I just smile for no reason; I'm sure strangers at airports or cafés must have thought I had gone mad. I love to smile, I smile at strangers and magic happens when a stranger smiles back at you. Not the creepy kind of smile, but the genuine smile that says I'm glad to see

you. I find smiling to be a great universal language. Sometimes you may never know what other people are going through or what they are thinking, but I know I'm not completely dressed if I leave the house without a smile.

8. *Opportunity.* Many times this comes in form of work. Like Steve Jobs said, "You can't connect the dots looking forward, you can only connect them looking backwards. So you have to trust that the dots will somehow connect in your future. You have to trust in something – your gut, destiny, life, karma, whatever." Opportunities in my life have come in the form of work. I always have to work hard and put a lot of effort in to accomplish anything in my life and this applies to many. Whatever position you are in right now, look at it as a stepping stone to your future and have the courage to do better than your best.

Chapter 11: You are Perfect with Your Imperfections

You Have The Power

1. Write down five things you love about yourself.

   _____

   _____

   _____

   _____

   _____

2. Write down five things you are great at doing.

   _____

   _____

   _____

   _____

   _____

3. What makes you different from everyone else?

   _____

   _____

   _____

   _____

   _____

Chapter 12:

Emotional Intelligence

> *"There are high spots in all our lives and most of them come about through encouragement from others."*
>
> **Unknown**

Back in Katete, my grandfather would sit with the family on most evenings after dinner in the sitting room by the fireplace and he would tell us stories. At the end of every story, my grandfather would ask what the moral of the story was.

My grandfather would tell us a story of a girl who was made out of wax. He would explain how her parents loved this special girl and that she had to live indoors as the hot African sun would cause her to melt. This girl made of wax obeyed her parents, but she had a strong desire to see what daylight was like. After spending many years in a cool hut by day and only going outside by night, the girl made out of wax finally went out when the sun was high in the sky, and she immediately melted into a pool of wax.

I Have the Power

Grandpa looked at us and asked, "What is the moral of the story?" One of my uncles said, "Listen to your parents or you will melt! " Grandpa looked at him, slightly disappointed. He explained to me the importance of understanding your limitations, your strengths and weaknesses, and how you can use them to help you in life. Once you fully understand who you really are, you can achieve greatness and grandpa would encourage us not to feel limited by the borders society has put upon us. Think outside the box to reach your true potential.

In my life, I have family, close friends, strong mentors and advisors, but they all let me think for myself and let me make my own mistakes; they will never judge me, at least not openly. I found that one of the most important things as a young social change-maker; I had to learn how to deal with my emotions. You will have days when you feel the earth should open up and swallow you, or maybe that's just way too drastic.

When I was young, I had to learn how to read peoples' minds through their eyes very quickly. That's why when you sit with me, I'll be looking you straight in the eye. They say the eyes are the windows to the soul. It's also an African thing to look people straight in the eyes to see if someone is telling the truth, and also as a sign of respect. Having spent a good number of years observing animal behaviour, I figured out it was a survival thing. I do not do this to intimidate anyone; it's a sign of respect from my culture. Nonetheless, I learned that my own response combined with the other person's response would determine the outcome. First, I had to learn how to express myself respectfully. If I felt that I had been treated unfairly at home, at school or any social group, I would make sure that I wrote the incident down. I would discuss the issue and do my best not to accuse anyone of anything. This helped me to deal with all sorts of tension and as an adult, I still use this

Chapter 12: Emotional Intelligence

technique. I also learned how to apologize for my part. Apologising is very hard for most people. Usually people say: "I'm sorry if I hurt you." That is not an apology: that is an excuse. There is nothing wrong with saying you are sorry. It won't take the pain away or the inconvenience you have caused, but it is a bridge between you and the other person. People need to learn to genuinely apologize and be able to acknowledge their mistakes.

My father is a classic example. Dad would never say he is sorry for anything; he will try to make up for the wrong he has done, but to get the words 'I'm sorry' out of his mouth is like trying to extract blood from a stone. As a family, we know that is how dad behaves and we have accepted that, but as his child, I would go to great lengths to test his limits until I would hear him apologize with words. This is not something I would recommend doing to someone you don't have a personal relationship with.

You should be able to read your own emotions and the emotions of those around you, and you should be able to understand why you are behaving the way that you do. By being aware of your emotions, you will be able to avoid many pitfalls. Your emotional Intelligence and awareness is based on your feelings. If you know what sets you off, you will also know how to deal with such issues when they arise. Knowing in advance how you will react to certain situations prepares you to make the best possible choices. For example, I know that I get nervous when I stand on stage in front of people, so I prepare myself physically, emotionally and psychologically. I visualise being on stage and giving my best performance ever. I even visualize people clapping or complimenting me. I also visualize the worst-case scenario, where someone says something to upset me. When this happens in reality, it wouldn't come as a surprise. I know that I don't tolerate nonsense and call a spade a spade, but I also know how it keep cool, calm and composed. How you express yourself

I Have the Power

matters; so how do you safely express your emotions without being misunderstood? Expressing myself without being too emotional is something I'm still learning.

I was coming from the Young Minds Conference when I had met and sat with His Holiness the Dalai Lama. I was pumped and happy. As I stepped into my taxi, the driver greeted me and helped me with my bags. I was heading back to Melbourne from Sydney, flying Virgin Airlines. Checking in was a breeze and I went straight to my gate with a big smile on my face. The security guard made a comment on how happy I looked, so I told him that I just had met the Dalai Lama earlier that day. I was just happy. As I was checking in on Facebook, I saw this guy, sitting across in the waiting lounge looking at me; I smiled at him and continued to play with my phone. I was one of the last to board, as I was flying economy. He was already in the plane, flying business.

As I walked past his seat, he was looking at me and I just smiled. I told myself that nothing could disturb my peace, so I went to my seat, buckled up and tried to read. I guess I must have been so extremely tired from all the fun in Sydney that I fell asleep as soon as the plane took off. To my surprise, I opened my eyes and the guy was sitting next to me. He was looking at me, smiling. At this point, I realized that I had probably given this guy a wrong message. The first thing he said was how pretty I was and that he wanted to be friends. Ok, when a guy comes on like that, it's a warning sign. Run! But having gone through the whole topic on dealing with people and emotions and how to reason, I thought it would be good if I could calmly explain why he could not have my number and why I did not want to be his friend. I realized that I was going to hurt this person, but it was just way too creepy for a stranger to move from his seat to come and plant himself next to me. After my comments, he went back to his seat.

Chapter 12: Emotional Intelligence

Once you develop the ability to manage your own emotions, you gain self-control and you are able to focus on the important things in life. For example, no matter how bad a day starts, if you have self-control, you can go through the day by changing the way you react to circumstances. People that have a strong ability of self-control or emotional resilience are able to cope with such situations without dragging everyone around them in their mood. You know how sometimes people can walk through the door and they are just emotional vampires, but if you have a strong will, no matter how grumpy they are, their mood won't affect you. As a young up-and-coming leader, in order for you to be successful in your chosen path, you will need to have taken time to learn more about yourself.

> *"The bottom line is that we have only ourselves to blame. We create our own destiny by the way we do things. We have to take advantage of the opportunities and be responsible for our choices."*
>
> **Robert Frost**

As a young social change-maker, I have had to make decisions about my life, my work and my relationships. Some of these decisions have not been easy. However, having the freedom to make a choice means that you can also make a wrong choice! But the moment you realise that you have made a mistake, turn around and do what is right. It all comes to matters of the heart; what makes you happy? When I was young, all I wanted to do was help people. I now realise that I cannot help people if I'm not empowered myself. Take the time to learn what it is that makes you happy. As a child, I was told that God has given all of us talents; some of these talents have not been properly developed and are often ignored, but your challenge is to realize these talents and use them to help you and those around you.

During one of the conferences I attended, a speaker mentioned that zero stress is very bad for you. He told the audience that we create stress by resisting force. How do you resist force, one might say? Well…

You have to realize what causes you certain stresses and then educate the other person. One example I'll give is about a common question people ask me when they meet me for the first time. Are you from Africa? The response is always, I was born in Africa, but I'm Australian. Then the conversation will go in the lines of, "Do you speak Afrikaans?" My response used to always be the same, an irritated "No." Then the person goes ahead to say, "But you're African, how come you don't speak Afrikaans?" After many years of going through this, I realized that it's not that the person is trying to irritate me, but they are trying to make a conversation and they don't know any better. Most people think Africa is a country with different states and that we are all the same with the same language. Sometimes people great me in Swahili, A language that is widely spoken in Africa, but not in the Southern African region, where I come from.

Persistence and patience are the two most important virtues one should have. Just get the work done and stop telling yourself stories as to why you didn't do what you had to do. Once you get into the habit of getting work done, life becomes a lot easier. You might say,

Chapter 12: Emotional Intelligence

"I don't have enough time," well, sleep less! Make other people look good—if you are working for somebody, make your boss look good. Often when we give genuine compliments to others, it makes them feel good and guess what, what goes around comes around. If you say nice things about people, they will say nice things back to you, even when you're not around, and it's hard for anyone to badmouth you if you are nice, as no one will believe them.

All the conferences that I attend are mainly for professional development, but I find that they have a common trend and I have time to focus on personal development. You cannot be the best at what you do if you are not taking care of yourself. You are only 1% of the solution; so to solve the problem you are trying to solve, get other people on board. From a very young age, I always understood that I couldn't make a change on my own. We have an African proverb that says, "One finger cannot lift the pot." Ask other people to help you solve whatever it is you want to do. Be it just reading through your project proposal or connect you with someone you would like to meet.

You Have The Power

1. How do you deal with emotions?

___

2. Write down five things you can do to stop you from exploding after someone has said or done something wrong to you.

___

3. List three things that make you happy.

___

Chapter 13:

Looking After Yourself Looks After the World

> "The greatest gift you can give to you is to completely love yourself."
>
> **Nkandu Beltz**

Make simplicity your passion: start by writing down your passion and put things you are passionate about in your diary. I learned that if I document what I want to achieve and set deadlines, I am more likely to actually achieve them. Simple things I have learned to do recently have taken me more than 20 years to master.

You have to learn to say no to people or activities that won't help you grow as a person. I found that I took on too much and I began to resent myself, as I did not have enough time for myself or the ones I truly love. It's like the story of the stones in a jar! The story tells about a professor giving a lecture about 'Efficient Time Management' to a group of executive managers. He filled a jar full of large stones and asked them if the jar was full. They all replied,

I Have the Power

"Yes." He then poured small pebbles in the jar, which filled big holes between the large stones up to the rim. He asked the question again and one manager answered, "Apparently not." "Correct," he said and continued to fill the small spaces in between the stones and pebbles with sand and filled it again up to the brim.

Now, all the executive managers answered the question with "No." "Correct," he said and filled the jar with water to completely fill it. He then explained the lesson from the experiment, "If we don't put all the large stones in the jar first, we will never be able to fit all of them later! What are the large stones in your life? Your Health? Family? Friends? Goals? Doing what you Love? Fighting for a Cause? Taking time for yourself? Remember, it is MOST important to include the large stones in our lives, because if we don't, we might miss out on life altogether! If we give priority to smaller things in life (pebbles and sand), there is not enough time for the important things in life! Never forget to ask yourself, "What are the Large Stones in MY Life?" and ensure they have enough space in your Jar of Life!

Make sure that you take care of the most important things in your life first! Laundry can wait unless, of course, you are up to your last underwear; spend quality time on yourself and those you care about. Sometimes I feel like I have to do everything myself. I grew up believing if you want anything done properly, do it yourself! But now I know that you don't have to do everything yourself! I came to a stage in my life where I wanted to be Superwoman; I would wake up extra early, do as much as I could and if I had a task that I couldn't do, I would spend time learning how to do it. The truth is, you can always ask for help, especially when you have kids or are caretaking. This can be emotionally and physically demanding. You are not meant to do it alone. Ask for help! It's ok; it's not a sign of weakness.

Chapter 13: Looking After Yourself Looks After the World

It's also easy not to eat properly; I sometimes fall in this trap of having breakfast on the go, a piece of toast with marmalade and a cup of tea. But now I've gotten into the habit of making sure I eat a proper breakfast! Mum always said, "Start with a healthy breakfast and drink plenty of fluids!" She meant water, herbal tea, or freshly squeezed juices. We never had fizzy drinks growing up. Ice cream was a treat; I loved soymilk and still do.

Taking care of your body is very important, but taking care of your mind is even more so. Take five minutes in the morning to centre yourself: this can be done through prayer, meditation or a gratitude list. Allow a few extra minutes to set your intentions for the day. Look at your 'to do' list and visualise what your day should look like. A 'to do' list is something my Entourage business coach, Clare Jennifer, encouraged. Colour code your priorities—do one thing at a time and do it correctly.

Don't forget about physical exercise. I remember when I was in high school; I used to come up with all sorts of excuses as to why I should not participate in sports. I would be happy to play basketball on certain days, but I was on the bench most of the time. I would go and play tennis a few times a month, but competitive sports are something I'm not good at playing. I find that as I condition my body, my mind is being conditioned, too. I can never commit to one type of exercise, so I would alternate among rowing, skipping, running and occasional swimming. You will never find me in the gym; the first and last time I was in the gym, I was confused and could not work out what I wanted.

I find that 'the great outdoors' works well for me. The beauty about exercising is that I feel better and I think more clearly. When you are physically and mentally fit, you can tackle any challenges that will come to you. As an important member of your community, you need to take care of yourself. You need to fuel your body with proper food and drinks. You need to make sure your muscles are conditioned properly and that your mind is conditioned and fed properly. What you put into your head is just as important as what you put into your mouth. I have accountability partners for my health. My friends will tell me when they think I'm over-indulging on chocolate; they are not afraid to tell me this because they know I trust them and they trust me.

Sometimes people say "We are eating comfort foods" (food you eat to feel better, like ice cream or French fries), but how comforting is it if it looks like a recipe for a heart attack? It's okay to once in a while eat that pizza, but you can also make your own pizza, your own wholemeal pancakes and homemade fruit juices. The Internet is full of healthy recipes that you can download and make at home. But the fact is, YOU have the power to choose what you put in your mouth. You have the power to set up an exercise plan and follow it for only 28 days. That's how long it takes to make a habit permanent as part of your routine. You have the power to do whatever you want that will help you move to the next level of your life, be it having a healthier body and mind, applying for a job, or going back to school to learn the skills you need.

Work on your connections. Keep your friends close and your loved ones even closer. Everyone is busy and we often don't find time to hang out with friends but a simple text message can make a big difference. For me it means: I'm here, I care and I'm your friend. I often send 'smileys' to my friends, just a simple reminder that I miss them or I'm thinking of them and that I value their friendship. Make sure you have time to switch off! Yes, from Facebook, Twitter, your mobile phone and all other distractions in your life. This is not an easy task to do, but most successful people have 'me' time. But don't create a 'me' time that lasts a lifetime, that's just egoistic and bad! My 'me' time is taking a warm bubble bath, listening to some beautiful classical music and just smiling. I encourage everyone to

Chapter 13: Looking After Yourself Looks After the World

keep a diary! This is how I keep track of my life and feelings.

Sometimes it feels like I'm moving in the fast lane and sometimes I miss out on what is happening, so on most days, I write down how I'm feeling about the activities of the day. What also works well for me is dressing in my favourite clothes. I'm a girl and I love to dress up—I will not apologize for that! When I look good, I feel good. I have certain colours that just instantly make me smile when I wear them. I love the quote in Dan Brown's novel *The Lost Symbol*: "The secret is in the order." My interpretation of this is being tidy. If everything is in order, it's easy to do everything. I find that when everything is neat and tidy, it's much easier to think clear and plan things. It's also easier to find things. It's ok to be a little messy, just not too extreme!

One of the lessons I learned was to outsource labour if you can. I don't want to spend time ironing my dresses if I can make more money being at the office or working on a project. But sometimes it's just great doing your own laundry. My point is, don't waste time learning bookkeeping when you can hire someone to do it for you! Delegate when necessary!

Another important aspect of looking after yourself is by making sure that you have financial literacy. We spend so much time learning and mastering everything that will not serve us any purpose in life and not paying enough attention to learning about money. I find that Australians are very lucky as most students are taught about money in school. When I was in school, I never learned any business skills, even though I would make fat cakes and sell them at recess so that I could make extra pocket money. In Australia, we have many places to learn about finance and planning your future so that you can be financially independent. One of the best pieces of advice I got was not to live beyond my means. Don't overspend money on wants. Follow your passion, exercise, eat healthy, drink plenty of water and be a good person; this world needs your kindness.

You Have The Power

1. What are your energy levels like at the moment?

___

2. What would it take to get into a consistent healthy eating and exercise habit?

___

3. Imagine yourself at the end of 28 days. How would you feel?

___

Chapter 14:

My Other Sources of Inspiration

> *"Many hands make light work."*
>
> **William Shakespeare**

In my journey as a young change-maker and lover of humanity, I have come across many inspiring individuals doing amazing work, I thought this would be a great time to mention a few that continue to be my source of inspiration. I have had countless interviews, conversations, and coffee and cupcake sessions while talking to young people about life, about why I do what I do, and being a lover of humanity. But the truth is, it's not about me, it's about you and what YOU can do. I realised that as much as I love doing what I do, I want to inspire you to do something great for yourself and your community.

Jon Dunchusky is highly talented and one of the most inspirational people I know and I highly admire his work. I met Jon at the Creative Innovation conference in Melbourne. I knew he had run a number of very successful ventures and I wanted to find out if he had a secret to his success. It turned out, Jon does not have any secrets or magic potions to his success; he has worked very hard to be where he is and he has made some very smart decisions along the way. The first day of the conference, I was just wondering how come certain people seem to be having a great time in their chosen career fields whilst others are struggling? At that moment at the Sofitel Hotel on Collins Street, I had an 'Aha!' moment: Life is not a competition! I'm not in a competition with anyone. I often asked myself why I wasn't succeeding fast enough, but the truth is, life is a journey and, like my grandmother used to say, "Life is like a journey going to the top of the mountain. You will meet obstacles along your path, but you have only two options, either go around it or over it, but whatever you choose, make sure you do it with a good attitude."

This good attitude is what I found in many successful people. Jon is definitely one person who is always smiling and happiness is infectious. When I get the chance to be friends or sit in the company of these happy individuals, I consider it an honour and privilege. Jon is co-founder of The Conversation Farm. I remember when I first heard him speak; I wished more people around the world would have access to his mind. Imagine what we could do if all the change-makers, dreamers and implementers came together. I realized that we had so much in common and we all want to make this world a better place. I presented to him the challenges I was facing with my project and how the funding was drying up. I had no other ideas for fundraising to run the project without looking like a beggar. Jon, originally from Canada, teamed up with the most creative minds to revolutionise the way charity works. I asked him to write 'Words of Wisdom' that I could share with you.

At a conference in California, he delivered a keynote presentation at 8am. Surprisingly, there were as many people sitting on the floor or standing at the back as sitting on chairs. The atmosphere was

Chapter 14: My Other Sources of Inspiration

phenomenal, he said. And whilst he said he could think that the room was packed with his Californian fan club, he suspected that the reality was that most of them were there to see this special guest speaker who was doing a double act with him.

"Claire Lyons is a friend and a colleague who used to have her hand on the philanthropic chequebook of a rather large international corporation. One of the largest, and one of the most forward-thinking of all international corporations, PepsiCo."

Over her time there, she developed a rather deep dislike of charities. Today, she thinks that most are mediocre and lack any sense of imagination. She is not an irrational charity-hater. No, rather she has spent a lot of time trying to effectively give away a lot of money. She has received proposals from an awful lot of charities, and met with many, many people who have pitched her. And she is not impressed. It is an opinion, as they say, grounded in experience.

And whilst I do believe that charities are core drivers of a better world, I believe that she has a point. Charities have become outdated. The creativity, passion and energy have become strangled by technique, process and systems. And organisations that are mandated to change the world have become among some of the most risk averse on the planet. Is it possible to break out of this mediocrity and unleash a new wave of creativity and passion to drive innovation and excellence? Yes. But only if shared value is accepted as the new norm.

Shared value, first coined by Michael Porter in his Harvard Business Review article, is about the paradigm of the non-profit and for-profit worlds collaborating for mutual benefit. It is not about philanthropy. It is not about charity. It is about the business of changing the world. Transforming causes and making real change is about more than simply the love of humankind. It is about aligning that love with a shared sense of value creation. Let us not forget that philanthropy represents only 2% of GDP. By aligning that 2% with the capital of the other 98%, you then have a real recipe for change.

Every passionate person who wanted to change the world and set up a charity did so to solve a problem, to right a wrong, not to fund programmes. Yet the modus operandi of charities today is to raise money to fund programs. Solving programs involves innovation, outside-the-box thinking and often changing business models. Start-ups solve problems. Institutionalised organisations do not. "There has never been a better time to change the world," Jon says, "And the way to do it is to do something remarkable. Something that creates really 'thick' value, that makes money, solves a problem and makes a real difference." As his friend Claire Lyons says, "Mediocrity does not change the world." The words may not seem like much but they are true; this is the best time to do something great with your life: if you are perfectly happy, help someone live their dream. You do not have to give up your entire life, but start small; start now.

I often work with youth from 12 to 19, most of whom have a sense of disempowerment. Some have told me they have no idea how to make a difference in other people's lives. These young people have so much potential and they can change so many things for the better. For example, eradicating poverty, ending homophobia, all topics like these must be addressed in high schools and youth should start taking action by joining community groups or organisations, which have the same vision and values. This is what I did before I was even 10 years old. Once you find what you are passionate about, everything falls into place. The reason why I have picked this age range is because I often go into schools and these are the young people I have been talking to, these are the young people that I was representing when I was a 'youth rep'.

Chapter 14: My Other Sources of Inspiration

Through my journey as a social change-maker, I have come to meet many great people, but I also lost friends and loved ones. In 2012, we lost two boys, 12 and 14 years old, to suicide in the East Kimberley. These deaths are preventable. Nothing in this world can be so bad that we can't solve the problems together as a people. A lot of the young people I worked with told me they felt disempowered and disengaged from mainstream education, but these are the labels that we have put upon them and when you tell people something frequently enough, they begin to believe it. I would encourage you to use your words wisely, especially when dealing with young people.

You Have The Power

1. Who inspires you?

   _____

   _____

   _____

   _____

   _____

2. What are some of your values that you can share with your community, class or friends?

   _____

   _____

   _____

   _____

   _____

3. Write down 10 things you love about yourself:

   _____

   _____

   _____

   _____

   _____

Chapter 15:

STEMSEL

> "The secret to unlocking your potential is recognising an opportunity and having the courage to use it."
>
> **Heddie Gouldberg**

> "Every child needs to learn how to code."
>
> **Richard Branson**

When I was representing Western Australia at the International Human Rights Day in South Australia, I was very fortunate to meet many amazing women and men working on so many different projects around the globe, from projects on providing clean water to remote villages to the reduction of infectious diseases; all of these projects were driven by people with a passion. One young man introduced himself and asked what I did. I explained to him what I did and never did I think that this young man would be a source of inspiration. Besmellah Mohammadi was born in Afghanistan. I call him 'Buzz Lightyear', which makes him smile. Bez spent a few years in Nauru with his parents. He witnessed so many things that young people his age should not be witnessing. I also met his father, who like Bez, is very hardworking, humble and cheerful.

Besmellah arrived in Adelaide from Afghanistan when he was seven years old. He said it was unforgettable time of his life having to go through a 'time warp' which is used to describe refugees suffering a sense of homelessness. He told me he is very still very grateful that STEMSEL gave him his friends a relief from the time warp.

Bez belongs to a club called STEMSEL. It was my first time hearing about this 'Science Technology Engineering Maths Social Enterprise Learning' project. He started his STEMSEL journey on a hot January day. It happened to be at the Royal Australian Air Force base in Edinburgh. There he met Squadron Leader Fernando Gonzalez. Mr. Gonzalez showed the group around the base and then showed them a model of an Orion surveillance plane. Bez and his peers were to add electronics to it. He mentioned it was his first day with STEMSEL. Along the journey, Bez learned many things and perhaps the most important had to do with his own background.

"People from a migrant and refugee background usually have a set system. They go to school, go to university and then get a job. It takes many years for them to start giving back. STEMSEL has given me a way to break this system and start giving back faster. Essentially we call this 'Refugees Giving, Not Taking' or RGNT," he said. Since year nine, Bez has been involved with the RGNT project and connecting it to his schoolwork. After school he would go to the

Chapter 15: STEMSEL

STEMSEL Foundation to integrate with the International students. All the hard work is starting to pay off.

Bez and his team at The STEMSEL Foundation Club have worked tirelessly to bring international students to study in Adelaide as a way of giving back to the community! Earlier this year, he and his team introduced 20 students from Beijing to study in Adelaide, which is worth $4 million to the local economy! He told me how proud he is to contribute to the community, especially at a time when Holden announced it would close down the car factory. "This is a big achievement for us refugee youth. The Lord Mayor and the Chairman of Study Adelaide are over the moon," he wrote to me. It has helped to boost my confidence. My family is so proud and joyful we can give something back to the community, which has given so much to us!

"With Holden closing, the economy is, no doubt, going to be weaker. But we are confident that we can find a solution to replace Holden. STEMSEL is all about working together, hence our motto 'Many Hands Make Light Work.'"

As a social change-maker and storyteller, I love listening to personal triumphs. Bez has been offered an apprenticeship in Parliament House when he turns 18. He received this offer from a Member of Parliament after he proved to Ministers, Opposition MPs and VIPs at a dinner function that if they held hands and focused on the LED lamp of a "Human Conductor" he made, their energy would light up the lamp. They were delighted to prove electronically a 500+ years saying (Shakespeare's time) that Many Hands Make Light Work!

I look forward to many more STEMSEL experiences, which will help more refugees to integrate and contribute to the socio-economic wellbeing of the community. I asked him to tell me more about it. I found out that it was a hands-on problem-solving fun-filled workshop for young people. This is one of the few clubs around the country teaching young people about science and technology. We have become consumers of technology but forgot to invest in creating new technology. The kids in the program learn how to build, design and program a micro-controller. These chips are found in cars, aeroplanes, water suppliers, cell phones and almost every part of our society.

In 2013, I had the honour of being one of the STEMSEL judges at the Royal Adelaide Show, one of Australia's biggest events. I guess each show must have a star and one of my favourite stars was an 11-year-old girl named Meave. Meave had won the most outstanding exhibit for 2012, didn't win overall, but she wasn't giving up and entered again in 2013. My first thought when I met this adorable young girl was "Wow, she will go a long way and definitely will be very important one day!"

Meave knew her periodic table, something that I had crammed only when I was in high school and did not pay much attention to! This girl knew the importance of all the elements. She knew about robotics and she could even make one. The most remarkable thing about this young lady was that she had invented items that were useful to her community. She enjoyed programming technology and learning how it all works. Peng Choo, who is the founder of STEMSEL, made this project possible because he wanted to help the African youth living in Adelaide, who had been in trouble for all kinds of reasons, to have something meaningful to do. The whole project has become bigger and better and is now getting a lot of community support.

The kids I mentor in the club have many bright ideas and they are destined for greatness. I don't do many practical things with them, but mostly act as a sounding board and an anchor. I sometimes go

Chapter 15: STEMSEL

to meetings with them when they are meeting community leaders. I go through the proposals and ask the tough questions that I know outsiders would ask. They are working towards promoting integration and bringing more students into the country by being ambassadors for various groups. The club is so diverse in terms of ethnic backgrounds that we almost cover the whole world, but they all have one goal and they work together as a family. That is one of the things I love most about the STEMSEL Club; I simply act as a mentor, but I secretly call myself a CEO (chief enabling officer).

> *"It's not how much we do, but how much love we put in the things we do."*
>
> **Mother Theresa**

Every time I see one of these young people winning, or succeeding at something, I feel the joy in my heart. I guess the spirit of Ubuntu lives on, we are all connected and we are all one. The lesson I learned from these young people is the persistence to try and keep on trying. No one said it would be easy, but it's always worth a try. No matter how often you fall, get back up and develop a new game plan and try again. You are only defeated when you give up.

After being exposed to STEMSEL, I heard about organisations like Robogals, a group of students bringing engineering, science and technology to schools in order to increase participation in the industry. You can start a movement with anything that you think will create value to the lives of others. Find out what the needs are for your community and go out and make it happen.

You Have The Power

1. What has been one of the fears you have had to overcome?

   _____

   _____

   _____

   _____

   _____

2. How did you do it?

   _____

   _____

   _____

   _____

   _____

3. Write down a list of five people who are important to you and why.

   _____

   _____

   _____

   _____

   _____

Chapter 15: STEMSEL

My other source of inspiration is a young man with a bright future, Huw Grano – STEMSEL Student Leader. When I first met Huw, I had no idea as to how I could help this young man. Huw is a second year student at the University of Adelaide, studying Mechatronic (Robotic) Engineering and Computer Science. His journey with STEMSEL began in mid-2013 when he began volunteering as an intern, mentoring younger students in the STEMSEL electronics and robotics workshops. He also volunteered at the Royal Adelaide Show STEMSEL competitions, where he was able to see the inventions of the students mentored. I was one of the judges for this project with Squadron Leader and engineer Fernando Gonzalez from the Royal Australian Air Force and creative thinker Dr. YKK, Graham Brand from the Royal Adelaide Show and Miroslav Kostecki -Technical Manager at eLabtronics.

STEMSEL is slowly building its momentum and people are realizing more than ever the importance of Science, Technology, Engineering and Mathematics and paying more attention to it with the likes of Barrack Obama and Richard Branson talking about it. I asked Huw to write about his experience and share what the club is doing on one of the subjects I'm passionate about.

At first, being a logically-minded engineering student, Huw didn't believe that linking the areas of technology – STEM and Social Enterprise Learning – SEL, could really work. However, as he became further involved in the project, he came to understand the unique value proposition that STEMSEL has for sustainable social and economic development, by finding and developing the inventors of the future amongst our younger generation. STEMSEL's effectiveness in achieving this goal lies in that it exposes children to STEM from a young age. Moreover, the STEMSEL workshop students, who may be as young as 10, are required to design their inventions aimed to solve social and economic problems in the community. As a social change-maker, I'm still in awe as to what this project can do to solve some of the social problems our communities are currently facing.

For example, the students may be asked to design a system to dim or brighten a streetlight, which reacts to the presence of oncoming cars; the aim of this being to reduce electricity usage.

This uses pulse width modulation – an engineering concept Huw recently learned at university! But kids are still able to learn this because STEMSEL students control the light with an easy to learn language. At the same time, their inventions are judged for social and economic impact, which might include environmental effects or economic impact under a carbon-trading scheme. By completing these sorts of projects, STEMSEL students have knowledge in technical engineering and its social impact far beyond their years by the time they reach university.

These STEMSEL-trained university students are then able to become interns in the Foundation, creating a sustainable cycle. The interns are actively involved in the running of the Foundation, whether this be in technical or business aspects and are mentored by industry experts. Students from the realms of engineering and business are able to work together to run workshops and organize new workshops at schools and councils. For many students involved in this project including Huw, this has been an invaluable experience because they have been able to learn practical business communication and networking skills. This empowers students to consider pursuing a career in the management or business aspects of engineering and develops self-confidence. Most importantly, this is how STEMSEL is developing employability skills amongst the younger generation, which are deficient amongst graduates across all fields.

Huw also visited a school in China as an intern of the Foundation and spoke to the students about the merits of studying in Australia

Chapter 15: STEMSEL

and career benefits from doing the STEMSEL Internship Programme. He thinks that quite a few Chinese students will actually come to Adelaide to study. In the future Huw believes STEMSEL will be a key organization in Australia's international student industry, bringing vital education export revenue to Australia.

You Have The Power

1. Find time to speak with a person from a different cultural background, make sure you are in a safe environment and ask sensible questions.

___

___

___

___

___

2. What are your current perceptions of refugees? Are they true?

___

___

___

___

___

3. What do you care about in terms of social justice?

___

___

___

___

Chapter 16:

(Shikoba)
I Exist For You

> "Only a life lived for others is a life worthwhile"
>
> **Albert Einstein**

Whatever relationship you are in, humans need to communicate in order to achieve something they want. Your communication skills are very important. You need to do your level best to express yourself in a respectful manner. When I was in grade five, my class teacher talked to us about our rights and freedom of speech. We interpreted that lesson to mean that we could just say whatever we wanted at any time. I remember going home with my brain loaded with thoughts of my rights as a girl child. I arrived home to a nice meal, which my mother had prepared.

After a long day at school, hungry and tired, only wanting something delicious to eat, my mother had prepared nshima with chicken and pumpkin leaves. Nshima is a staple food in most African countries and it looks like potato mash but has a blunt taste. This is where the

I Have the Power

chicken comes in handy; Mum has a way of cooking her food: she shallow-fries the chicken, making it crisp just on the outside, then makes a relish dish with fresh veggies and herbs and a few spices. She then adds the mixture to the chicken and serves it with nshima and very green leafy veggies. This is food for the soul. I can eat nshima and chicken anytime.

As I finished my meal, I left the table and went to my room; this was a behaviour that shocked my parents. Dad called me back and asked if I was ok; I said yes, just a bit tired. He asked why I did not thank my mother for such a lovely meal. Mum made lovely meals all the time, but it was just a tradition to thank the cook in the house. I said thank you for cooking us such a beautiful meal. As I walked away, Dad asked about the dishes; who was going to wash them? I said, "Dad, cleaning up is a violation of my rights! I'm a child and children don't clean up!" Dad looked at me and smiled. "You learned about rights today?" I said "Yes!" "Did your teacher talk to you about responsibilities as well?" I looked at him, puzzled, with a "Huh?" He said, "Daughter, you have rights and you are free to express those rights anytime, but you also have responsibilities. 'Rights' come with 'responsibilities'."

Freedom has a price. So when you go out there and you are expressing yourself, make sure you are not intimidating anyone. The way you say things is very important, how you say it and how you make other people feel when you say it does matter. Sometimes we say things that could hurt other people, so we have to be mindful of what we say. The expression on your face matters as well. People are smart and can detect a phony smile a mile away. Be your authentic self. Dress the way you feel like and act like you, not anyone else.

When it comes to communication, find out what works for you. I know I am very good with one-on-one conversations, but put

Chapter 16: (Shikoba) I Exist For You

me in a room with seven or more people, and I become very self-conscious. But I know that communication is one of my strengths; put me in a room with hundred or even a thousand people, and I'll be fine. I know that even though English is my third language, I can speak confidently and express myself clearly.

Work on your written skills, too! It's very important to write and spell correctly. The first book I ever published was a series of poems and I did not put much focus on spelling. The publishing house I used did not do a spell check and when the book came out, I was shocked about the number of spelling mistakes. I should have given it to someone for proofing. Having English as a second or third language is not an excuse for poor grammar. Learn to communicate effectively in whatever language you use. One of my favourite poems, written by Rudyard Kipling, sums up my whole life in a good way and I'm sure this resonates with you. I came upon that poem when I was in secondary school.

If

If you can keep your head when all about you

Are losing theirs and blaming it on you,

If you can trust yourself when all men doubt you,

But make allowance for their doubting too;

If you can wait and not be tired by waiting,

Or being lied about, don't deal in lies,

Or being hated, don't give way to hating,

And yet don't look too good, nor talk too wise;

I Have the Power

> *If you can dream---and not make dreams your master;*
> *If you can think---and not make thoughts your aim;*
> *If you can meet with Triumph and Disaster*
> *And treat those two imposters just the same;*
> *If you can bear to hear the truth you've spoken*
> *Twisted by knaves to make a trap for fools,*
> *Or watch the things you gave your life to, broken,*
> *And stoop and build 'em up with worn-out tools:*
> *If you can make one heap of all your winnings*
> *And risk it on one turn of pitch-and-toss,*
> *And lose, and start again at your beginnings*
> *And never breathe a word about your loss;*
> *If you can force your heart and nerve and sinew*
> *To serve your turn long after they are gone,*
> *And so hold on when there is nothing in you*
> *Except the Will which says to them: 'Hold on!"*
> *If you can talk with crowds and keep your virtue,*
> *Or walk with Kings---nor lose the common touch,*

Chapter 16: (Shikoba) I Exist For You

> *If neither foes nor loving friends can hurt you,*
>
> *If all men count with you, but none too much;*
>
> *If you can fill the unforgiving minute*
>
> *With sixty seconds' worth of distance run,*
>
> *Yours is the Earth and everything that's in it,*
>
> *And---which is more---you'll be a Man, my son!*
>
> *(Kipling 1943)*

When you are in the public eye, not everyone will appreciate you. You will find people who will criticize you for anything, including the way you walk. You need to know that in life, things never stay the same. Your body will change, your friends will change and you will have new friends as you grow older, as values and vision might not be aligned anymore. Your community changes all the time. My thinking changes also as you learn and experience things. What I know now, shapes my thoughts. You need to be flexible in your thinking! When I became a girl child advocate, I thought it was my responsibility to make sure that each and every girl child in Zambia was safe and had access to education with the three basic needs for a child to survive, food, clothing and shelter. But the truth is, I did my best but it takes a generation to change things and make things better and that generation could be my generation!

I dedicated my entire youth years to this cause, but as time went by, things began to change and now as a grown woman, I know that I cannot do this alone. I need help; the human race needs to work as a team to improve the situation with the girl child problems in

I Have the Power

most Third World countries. This is not a problem for Zambia alone, this is a problem that affects us all; it's a global problem. Recently I was reading about a girl form Somalia who left the comforts of a developed nation, Canada, to go back to her home country. She returned to help her mother, who was running a not for profit organisation, helping girls and women, who have been abused. She assisted set up housing for them and providing a place of refuge. She talked about how they now have an open dialogue with the Somalian government about such issues. She is not doing it alone. She has systems put in place that help her to be of significance to her people. It's not your responsibility to change the world, just be yourself and do what you can. If you do your part, that is enough.

Brene Brown explains 'empathy' really well. Quite often when friends or family are going through tough times, we want to solve their problems. I have been guilty of this habit. Instead of listening quietly and empathising, we are too quick to offer solutions. Most of the time, the person telling you their problem, just wants you to listen. Sometimes all you have to say is: "I can't feel what you are feeling but I'm sure it's tough for you." We have to stop pretending that we know what other people are going through. You can never feel my loss or my broken heart, but you can empathise with how I'm feeling.

In Africa we have a proverb that says, "Only the pot knows how hot the water is". It is very important to listen without interrupting, without judging and accepting people as they are. The best thing you can do for another person is listening patiently to their stories of love, dreams and problems. Even though you have been there, done that and got the T-shirt, just accept them. As an important member of your community, people will confide in you; they will come to you for advice and you will have to trust and build relationships with people.

Chapter 16: (Shikoba) I Exist For You

See things from different perspectives – not just a broader ego perspective, but go to the roots and see things from a closer point of view, question things, ask why, don't be content with the way things are. When I went on my first retreat at Commonground with seventeen other Young Social Pioneers from around Australia, I thought I knew myself quite well. How I was mistaking! The retreat was a great time to learn about being your authentic self. The program was great and it taught me how to read and understand people. We did a personality leadership style test to find out how we look at life in general and how we are likely to solve problems. I came out as a 'Deer'; the lady that was running the workshop based the results on American animals. I was very surprised by the results as I thought I had a broader overview of life. The main characteristics were that I was down to earth and very caring. Sometimes it just helps to support people and let them shine. We cannot all be stars; we need someone to support these stars to shine. This does not make you less significant! Behind every great man there is a woman as they say! I'm not sure if the opposite goes for great women too….

It is very important to look at things from different angles. A view from the top will be different from a view from the bottom. You have to ask yourself why things are the way they are. One of the lessons I remember clearly was about 'dropping the mask'. I didn't realize that everyone wears a mask. We put it on first thing in the morning and take it off at bedtime. When we introduced ourselves, we were asked to do it in the most authentic way. Anyone who knows me will tell you how I love to smile. Every time I would go on stage, I would flash a smile but the instructor asked me to go back three times and drop the smiling mask. This confused me greatly as that is who I am. So out of embarrassment I put my frowning mask on and said my name.

The importance of this lesson was that once you know who you are

I Have the Power

and realize why you do what you do, you are able to go out there and face the world. It was a good lesson and from that time on, I would look in the mirror and ask myself, "Who is Nkandu?" Society has an idea of who you should be, how you should behave and how you should dress, but you make the rules and you are the one who needs to come up with a game plan as to how you will live your life.

So we now know that in order to succeed at any time, you need to put in your best effort, have very good work ethics and have a master plan. You to need to simplify your dream and the most important question you should be asking yourself is 'Why?' Why do you want to do this? Why have you set these goals? It does not matter who you are and where you stand in life.

Success has to do with personality and attitude; you must have the flexibility to shift your thinking perspective and keep your eyes on the goal. This applies to all aspects of our lives; our attitude towards life, work and our relationships determines our successes and failures.

You have to be very observant and learn from what others are doing and definitely do not be afraid to ask for advice. Get skilled people to help you with implementation of your ideas. Do what is important first. How do you actually put this in a formula that works for you? You must always have a clear 'why' and stick to it! You should not be carried away by new trends. Have the courage to follow your own path. Do not be a people-pleaser! Believe in something, make a choice and stick to it, then actually do it.

Relationships are important to me, and I cannot emphasise enough how grateful I am to the people around me. I have been very fortunate to be mentored by the likes of James Gardner from UBS and Nicky Carp from UHG. These relationships came about through Foundation for Young Australians when I was selected as a Young

Chapter 16: (Shikoba) I Exist For You

Social Pioneer in 2012. My relationship with my mentor James has always been great; he has taught me so much. He went out of his way to introduce me to people who would help me move my Youth Empowerment Program Australia (YEPA) forward.

I regret that I did not spend more time listening to my mentors. James was able to use his business skills to advise me on how to shape the future of YEPA, and had told me that he'd had a very good mentor at some point in his life himself. Despite being an Associate Director at UBS, one of the worlds' most successful and biggest financial institutions, I found James to be a 'down to earth' guy.

I was also very fortunate to have Nicky Carp as my other mentor. Nicky is gorgeous and calls a spade a spade and not a big spoon. Nicky and James brought in so much value and meaning to the things I was doing. I would sit down with Nicky and James and go through the program to discuss my values and focus points. One thing I should have done better was to focus on one thing only instead of trying to change the world with lots of projects on my table; I guess that is a lesson we all have to learn at some point in our lives: to focus is the key to success.

One thing I love about being the founder of YEPA is the ability to sit in a room full of young people, talking about the future, discussing the challenges that they face and trying to come up with solutions to these problems. Some youngsters that I worked with have shown tremendous leadership skills and courage to tackle some of the world's most pressing issues, from environmental sustainability to social justice. One day I will go back to communities like Rainbow, Nhill and Dimboola, to find out what happened to the kids I worked with: was their voice heard? How are their great ideas on how to keep youngsters occupied implemented and have their dreams of ways of contributions to their communities materialized? In an interview with Ana Cadorsa from FYA, she asked me what I was gaining from running this youth initiative. My response was 'personal growth'.

It's a selfish thing to say, but what makes me happy is seeing other people happy. If I can make someone around me happy, then I'm content with life. Every person that comes in my life gives me an opportunity to learn from him or her. That's why I try to maintain my relationships as much as I can, but there are times when you have to let go of the ones that are not doing you any good.

My mentoring experience through FYA was way above my expectations. I'm not afraid to ask questions, and sometimes it might sound stupid to ask certain questions, but I'm not afraid of being judged or labelled. One of my teachers once said that there is no such thing as a stupid question! When I was growing up, my family nicknamed me "Plunger". I'm the type of person who is not afraid to take risks but recently, I found that I was overanalysing everything and I might have missed out on great opportunities in life. The disadvantage of being a plunger is that you jump into decision-making but like my friend Jack Delosa says, "Trying and failing is better than not trying at all."

One important lesson I learned from my mentors was to live a balanced life. Anyone can have a balanced life once the right systems are put in place. Mentors are not meant to be friends; they are here to guide and help us to reach our goals. They are not paid and they do this out of interest and good will. I do mentor a few young people myself and I find that this is rewarding. I learn so much from them.

Chapter 16: (Shikoba) I Exist For You

You Have The Power

1. What are your aspirations for the next 12 months?

   _____

   _____

   _____

   _____

   _____

2. Write down three names of people who can help you reach your goal.

   _____

   _____

   _____

   _____

   _____

3. Write down five qualities of people you admire.

   _____

   _____

   _____

   _____

   _____

Chapter 17:

Nkandu's Cultural Night

> "No matter how bad you think your life is, wake up each day and be thankful for what you have. Someone, somewhere, is fighting just to survive."
>
> **Unknown**

My grandfather used to call me a storyteller. Every morning when I woke up, I would walk straight to the dining room where I knew he would be sitting, drinking his tea or finishing up breakfast. During the weekdays he would be wearing an old-fashioned tweed jacket and he would always look at me with a smile, as if it was the first time he had seen me. I would greet him with a kind of "Good morning," but the direct translation from Bemba, the language usually spoken in our house, was, "Have you woken up well today?'" He would smile and say, "Yes, we have woken up very well today." With this kind of response, nothing could go wrong! The day already had a great start and we just had to continue to add more blessings to it.

My grandpa often asked me about my dreams. He would say to me, "Nkandu, dreams are very important, they tell us about the future." He would then stop me from scratching my head before I told him the dream, as I would otherwise forget it. I would then tell him my dream in great detail. I would tell him what happened, the emotions I felt, the colours as if describing a movie and the mood of the people participating in my dream. I would talk for about 10 minutes while he would be sipping on his tea. When I finished, I would be standing next to him and looking at him. He would smile and say, "So Nkandu, tell me, what is the moral of the story?"

I would look at him with an 'I don't know' face, shrugging my shoulders in my pink pyjamas with the love hearts, which I wore for over five years. Most of the time, my dreams consisted of falling; sometimes I would be swimming or riding a bicycle in the streets naked and I was never bothered at all. Some of them were about me having long walks by the beach or climbing a mountain. Grandpa would say, "These dreams are telling you something; you have to act upon them." Even without the entire dream, my grandfather still managed to interpret it. Little did I know that one day I would realize, that all what life is composed of, are dreams and that it's up to us to make these dreams come true.

After I moved to Australia, a land I had only imagined as a young girl, little did I know that everything I had done in my life, would affect me. When I was watching the local television and the report was about the drought in Africa, I knew this was not a dream and I had no need to interpret it but simply had to act on it. Around August of 2011, one of the worst droughts ever hit Africa. Millions of people are still facing severe hardship and starvation due to the

Chapter 17: Nkandu's Cultural Night

prolonged drought. People are still forced to walk hundreds of miles without food and water to seek assistance in refugee camps.

Thousands of people are still dying, including children. One day I browsed through some TV channels and suddenly saw little malnourished children in a camp: the headline: East African Emergency Appeal. These words stuck in my heart and I could not get the image of the kid, virtually only skin and bones, looking straight into the camera. I felt this child was looking at me! Suddenly, I realised that that child could have been me! That could be MY child; that could be anyone I know and I felt this immerse urge to do something. I always have a partner in crime: I called Erik and said, "I'm hosting a bigger and better Cultural Night and this time, all funds raised will go straight to Save the Children Australia, as they have a Children's Emergency Fund." Besides, I had worked with STC and I know how much work they do to help children. I made a few phone calls and asked STC if they would be ok with me doing the fundraising. That was no problem; I was immediately given the go-ahead.

I realized I would need help; a mastermind team, so I called Jacinta Thompson, Maria Chan, Emily Bolto, Nicci Reed and Gary Gaffney, the man who can perform miracles in the East Kimberley. I drafted the following letter:

Good Morning,

As I am sure you are aware, millions of people in East Africa are currently facing severe hardship and starvation due to the prolonged drought. People are being forced to walk for days without food or water to seek assistance in refugee camps. Children are dying and I can no longer bear to see the faces

> *of little children on the news without trying to do something about it. I believe that if we all work together, we can have some impact.*
>
> *For some time now, I have been holding 'Cultural Nights' in Kununurra. The idea behind these nights is to celebrate cultural diversity in our community. Each family is encouraged to bring a plate of food from their traditional country or hometown to share with other participants.*
>
> *To really get into the spirit, guests should come dressed in their traditional attire. We will share different traditional dances and songs from Australia and around the world.*
>
> *This year I would like to make this event meaningful by giving raised funds to STC to support the refugee children in East Africa.*
>
> *On Sunday evening, the 25th of September, at 5:00pm, I will be holding the next 'Cultural Night'. The staff at Zebra Rock Gallery has generously joined in with this cause and offered us their venue!*
>
> *Yours sincerely,*
>
> *Nkandu Beltz.*

This letter got a lot of support and within minutes of sending it, I had more than a 100 emails in my inbox. I received all kinds of suggestions how to go about the event, offers of assistance and an interview with ABC local. I guess I was not the only person affected by the images on TV, but the most overwhelming feeling was the

Chapter 17: Nkandu's Cultural Night

sense of community and togetherness that I felt. I could feel the essence of Ubuntu right here in Australia.

Lee-Ann Dyson spent many hours to create a cake that was later auctioned and enjoyed by one lucky family. Local companies donated items for auction, door prices were donated, airtime on local radio stations and advertising space so that we could raise more money. We received food for the evening and had Chef Jasper Kroes to cook for the guests. This was the best event I ever hosted and the community of Kununurra was truly amazing. I could not have done this by myself.

Bruce and Diana Livett from Zebra Rock Art Gallery put in so much effort to make this a fantastic event. I had the team from Save the Children working around the clock to make sure that everything was in place. We had someone drop off a PA system. The community came in left, right and centre. The night was colourful; we began with Kiri and her belly dancing team. We had a children's choir with songs from the Lion King with masks on. A lady had approached me, asking if she could do a traditional Japanese dance. She did an amazing job, wearing traditional Japanese cloths with a beautifully coloured 'umbrella'. I ran a 'tying the headscarf' competition, in which guests were shown once how to put a traditional South African scarf on and then had to make the best of it themselves on male volunteers from the crowd! The winner actually did a fantastic job, better than I would! One of my favourite items on the program was the 'African Quiz'. It's quite surprizing how many people think that Africa is a country! We then had a PowerPoint presentation on the situation in East Africa before finishing with the auction of donated items.

All this was made possible because of the support from local enterprises like Alligator Airways, Travel World, Mount Romance,

I Have the Power

The Country Club, Tuckerbox IGA Kununurra, Coles Kununurra, MG Corp and B Visual Media. I was and still am very proud to say that that event was very successful, raising much-needed funds and entertaining a large local audience (actually also including a large group of tourists from all over Australia). I believe that in this day and age, children should not be dying of hunger and preventable diseases. As a human race, it is our duty to help each other. It was wonderful to see so many cultures helping families they have never met. You, too, have the power to mobilise people to raise awareness for a cause that you care about.

All this was fun, but most rewarding was meeting a midwife who had been working in East Africa in a refugee camp and hear her talk about how the emergency supplies actually helped children. I met this lady during CHOGM in Perth who talked about the challenges they were facing working in difficult conditions. As long as you can communicate effectively, you have the power to do amazing things. For Cultural Night, I must admit that I was very scared. I was afraid that people might not turn up. I feared that something would go wrong, but my gut feeling was telling me it was ok to be afraid and ok to just give it a go! At least I could say that I did my best.

One of my heroes, Eleanor Roosevelt (1884-1962) paved the road not only for women, but also for the whole of humanity. I admire her courage to organise Democratic Women to help her husband Franklin to be elected as Governor. That was in 1928 and then he went on to become President of the United States four years later. She had a vision: she had a mastermind team to her make her vision reality. When she was a delegate at the United Nations, she shaped the Universal Declaration of Human Rights! She mentioned that every experience in life shapes your character:

Chapter 17: Nkandu's Cultural Night

> *"You gain strength, courage and confidence by every experience in which you stop to look fear in the face."*

These words are still true today! We have to recognise fear and we should be able to rise above it to pursue our reasonable goals and dreams.

You Have The Power

1. Make a list of your skills and talents. Then, write down how you can help other people with your skills and talents. What could you do for the world?

___

___

___

___

2. How do you think you will feel after you have helped that person/group?

___

___

___

___

___

3. List five names of people who can be on your mastermind team and come up with a plan to get them on board.

___

___

___

___

Conclusion

> *"You must be willing to block out anything that distracts you and run the race with your eyes on the goal."*
>
> **Unknown**

You are very fortunate that you have freedom; you have the freedom to choose who you want to be and what you want to be. However, having the freedom to make a decision also means that you are also free to make a wrong choice. When this happens, the best thing to do is seek forgiveness, learn from the mistake and start all over again, but this time, do what you know is right. You must always remember that you have the power to change the world, but that it first starts with you. You are created with a lot of potential and achieving this requires you to set goals for yourself and to take steps towards fulfilling them.

You will need to practice self-discipline, but you also need to be able to change your plans if they are not working for you. You will need to have strategies in place, but never be afraid to ask for help. Get others on board to help you achieve your dream. You need to set you standards high and never settle for anything less. Split your goals into achievable chunks. Imagine what your life should look like in five years, three years and then down to one year. In order to achieve this, you need to set up a day-to-day and week-by-week plan, which adds up to your five-year plan.

I do this myself in all aspects of my life, personal or business, but as we all know, sometimes life does not go the way we plan it. Circumstances change, but you should never be too discouraged to focus on your vision. You must have the courage to do better than your best.

> *"Whenever you set your task for your day, swallow the frog first."*
>
> **Jack Delosa**

What Jack meant was: start with the most important tasks of your day! Facebook can wait; start by finishing all the hard, scary or boring stuff. The people you associate with have a huge impact on the quality of the life you lead; this applies physically as well as emotionally. If your friends or colleagues do not serve you any purpose, don't be afraid to make new friends who *do* share your vision and dreams. Being ambitious and joining the ranks of professionals in any field is a great start. Don't wait for tomorrow, start were you are and do it now.

During your quest to change the world, helping others along the way will be part of it! Never delay in helping a person because you think you are not ready. You have many talents and skills that you

Conclusion

can use to help those around you. If you are short on time, little acts of kindness once in a while will do. Imagine if we all cared for each other and were a little kinder to others? This world would surely be a better place for everyone.

Life will knock you down, but it's not about how hard you fall, it's about how long it takes you to get up. I could have easily given up because it was too hard or because I could not speak proper English or the morning was too cold to get out of bed. The truth is, you have the power to unlock your potential to change your world. Create that vision board and turn your dreams into reality. And remember to do it with a good attitude.

Twice I had severe malaria and both times I thought I would die. I was so sick that most of the time, I had no idea what was happening to me. At these times, I realized how much I wanted to live; how much I loved life and wanted to be strong and healthy. Despite all the challenges that life will throw at you, you will bounce back because that is just your nature. If the spirit is strong, so will the body be. Life is for living and at the end we all die, but like Steve Jobs said:

> *"Live each day as if it was your last, because one day it will certainly be."*

Having this realization and being close to death several times, I have come to appreciate my life and I wake up every morning with a sense of gratitude. How do we grow to be a good person? This has been a question asked by many souls for a very long period of time. To become a good person is a personal choice. You have to decide who you want to be and what you want to be and work towards that. A good person is perfectly happy with his or her own imperfections. I'm a good person; I'm not perfect, but I do my best to treat others with respect and dignity. The human body has three basic needs: food, shelter and clothing (and added to that list by my young sister: Wi-Fi).

An environment conducive for growth is necessary to grow a good person, but you need to know who you are and you need to have inner peace. Gratitude is very important; be grateful for everything in your life, including the things that seem challenging as they are building you up for greater things. Like they say, with great power comes great responsibility. A supportive relationship is a must, it doesn't necessary have to be your mum or best friend, but find what works for you. You need to show compassion and empathy. Like Carla Rinaldi says, "I cannot be fine if you are not fine." That is very true. This world needs happy people; this world needs you.

Young people often ask me, "What can I do to make a difference; I'm only a teenager?" Well, my friend; that is the right question. Find out what your passion is, you can lend your voice, time, skills and talents to so many causes in your school or community. Even volunteering at a local club or helping to walk your neighbour's dog is a great way to start. What impact do you want to have on this planet? I want to be remembered as "the girl who inspired youth to make better choices in life and follow their dreams."

One of my favourite quotes is from his Holiness the Dalai Lama. He says, "If you think you are too small to make a difference, trying sleeping in a room with a mosquito." You have the potential to do so much, one way to start is by being kind to yourself, speak only good things about yourself, learn to appreciate yourself. Like Nelson Mandela once said, "By letting your own light shine, you

Conclusion

automatically give others permission to shine." It starts with you. Once you are happy with yourself, once you treat yourself with respect and dignity and are your authentic self and living up to your highest standards, others will begin to follow.

This is one of the greatest changes you can make for mankind. From there, you can help in your own household, school and community. You can join community groups that are safe uphold the same values as you. You can campaign for ideas that you support. I'm a big fan of volunteering, but there comes a time in your life that you have to make sure you have the balance between making a living and volunteering. You have to look after yourself as well.

"Many people are talented, yet a few distinguish themselves; the ability to rise above lies more in effort than talent". Like Geoff Colvin once wrote, talent is overrated. Whatever your dream is (provided it's a constructive dream), you can achieve it by putting in a 101% effort.

You can be whoever you want to be. When I was young, I aspired to be like Maureen Nkandu. She was then a local news anchor, but I knew I wanted to do more. I wanted to change people's lives for the better; to be the support they needed. When you conduct yourself with respect and have respect for others, you will have a massive influence on people around you. When you strongly believe in yourself and your cause, you will be able to influence others. All you need is the first follower. Share who you believe yourself to be today, what you do, why you do it, and what kind of woman you have become. You will inspire them, as you are amazing and it will help them to personally connect and relate to you; you can speak on their level.

I'll leave you with a lovely quote from a remarkable young man Sjon

I Have the Power

Kraan, he always says to me "

Enjoy your life; life is great! J

Acknowledgments

I would like to pass my sincere gratitude to my love Erik Beltz, you have been my rock and everything that a girl could need. I value your support. I would also like to thank my entire family. My mum and dad (Ethel and Henry Nshindano). I would have loved for my best friend and cousin Ruth Chungu to be holding this copy and reading it to me while we are eating ice cream on a cold and rainy day. I know you are looking down on me smiling. I miss you. To my late Aunty Bertha Mwale, who put so much effort into helping me be the girl that I am today. My teacher of English, Mr. Conteh, who said I should learn some more English, here's to you. I think I'm doing pretty well, thank you so much for your support when I needed it.

A very special thanks you to Jan Owen, whom I secretly call Mama Jan, a solid foundation and great mentor who have supported me professionally and personally. And the team at Foundation for Young Australians. I would also like to thank the following individuals for supporting me and being there when I needed them: Gary and Sue Gaffney, Judy Hendrikse, Heddie Goldberg, James Gardiner, Nicky Carp, Amanda Wilson, Jodie Puckle, Felicity Whorlow, Tea Maherl, Sissay Dinku, Shillar Sibanda, Jon Dunchusky, Huw Grano, Busmiller Mohammed and Bruce Livett.

My sincere gratitude goes to Alexander Valchev for the book cover design, Cheeky Monkey Photography Horsham for the cover photo, The African Community of Australia, Foundation for Young Australians, STEMSEL Club Adelaide, United Nations Association of

Australia-WA, Zebra Rock Art Gallery and the Kununurra Community. Also, I would love to send a big 'thank you' to all my social network followers @beltz-nkandu and Nkandu Beltz Facebook.

I have missed out some names on this list, but I truly appreciate your support to make this project a reality. Thank you very much. I would like to thank you for buying and reading my book and I truly hope you will benefit from it. Last but not least, my three adorable darlings, Michelle, Claire and Erik Tatenda. I love you and thank you for loving me unconditionally. Your love is amazing, I can't ask for more.

About The Author

Nkandu Beltz

Nkandu Beltz was born in Zambia, lived in four countries, and was named a Young Social Pioneer in 2012 by the Foundation for Young Australians. In 2013, she was a Creative Innovation Scholarship winner and Ambassador for the Unleashed Youth Summit. Nkandu has been a change-maker from a very young age. She initially started out as a girl child advocate and has served as an advocate for equal rights and raised awareness of HIV/AIDS. Nkandu has a background in journalism and news writing and has worked for the *Ngami Times* in Botswana and Warringarri Aboriginal Radio Station in Kununurra, as well as produced content for ABC open rural in WA.

I Have the Power

In June 2013, Nkandu was invited to interview his Holiness, the Dalai Lama, during the Young Minds Conference. In 2011, she was chosen to be an Australian Youth Representative at the Commonwealth Heads of Governments Meeting. Nkandu is very passionate about youth development and helping those in need. She has worked with Save the Children Australia and the United Nations Association of Western Australia.

Nkandu is the founder of Nkandu's Cultural Night and developer the Kununurra Youth Development Programme (KYDP). After noticing a lack of opportunities for integration of indigenous and non-indigenous youth in Kununurra, Nkandu was inspired to create a program offering skills to youth and promoting integration within the community.

Nkandu, alongside KYDP, developed projects that have been very successful in the community. Her programs covered an array of sectors from media arts to creative arts in an aim to break social and cultural barriers between young people. Nkandu is now based in Horsham and KYDP has evolved into a national program, Youth Empowerment Programme Australia. It provides skills-based mentoring projects and workshops that are creative, innovative, sustainable, and scalable in media arts, creative arts, performing arts, and professional and personal development.

To book Nkandu as a keynote speaker or as an MC at your function, please go to www.nkandubeltz.com.au or send her an email bnkandu@y7mail.com.

www.ingramcontent.com/pod-product-compliance
Lightning Source LLC
Chambersburg PA
CBHW070609300426
44113CB00010B/1474